G K Chesterton was born in London in 1874 and was educated at St Paul's School. He became a journalist and began writing for *The Speaker* with his friend Hilaire Belloc. His first novel, *The Napoleon of Notting Hill,* was published in 1904. In this book Chesterton developed his political attitudes in which he attacked socialism, big business and technology and showed how they become the enemies of freedom and justice. These were themes which were to run through his other works.

Chesterton converted to Catholicism in 1922. He explored his belief in his many religious essays and books. The best known is *Orthodoxy,* his personal spiritual odyssey.

His output was prolific. He wrote a great variety of books from biographies on Shaw and Dickens to literary criticism. He also produced poetry and many volumes of political, social and religious essays. His style is marked by vigour, puns, paradoxes and a great intelligence and personal modesty.

Chesterton is perhaps best known for his Father Brown stories. Father Brown is a modest Catholic priest who uses careful psychology to put himself in the place of the criminal in order to solve the crime.

Chesterton died in 1936.

GU00577974

G K CHESTERTON

William Cobbett

HOUSE OF
STRATUS

This edition published in 2008 by House of Stratus, an imprint of Stratus Books Ltd., 21 Beeching Park, Kelly Bray, Cornwall, PL17 8QS, UK.

www.houseofstratus.com

Typeset, printed and bound by House of Stratus.

A catalogue record for this book is available from the British Library and the Library of Congress.

ISBN 0-7551-165-3-4

Contents

I

THE REVIVAL OF COBBETT

This chapter is here called 'The Revival of Cobbett.' As originally planned, only a little while ago, it was to have been called 'The Neglect of Cobbett.' It is not unimportant to realise how recent has been the change. It is but a year or two ago that I had the great and (it is to be feared) the undeserved honour of reading a paper on the subject to the Royal Society of Literature on my admission to that body, which certainly consists almost entirely of men who know much more about literature than I do. It was a graceful formality on such an occasion for the least learned person in the room to lecture to all the rest. Yet on that occasion the chairman, who was much more of a literary expert than I am, remarked on my having chosen an obscure and largely forgotten writer, just as if I had been lecturing on one of the last and least of the Greek sophists, or one of the numberless and nameless lyrists among the Cavaliers. Between then and now the change from neglect to revival has taken place. It is true that it is not until the first beginnings of the revival that we ever even hear of the neglect. Until that moment even the neglect is neglected. When I delivered the highly amateur address in question, the memory was already stirring, in others besides myself. But it is not out of egotism that I give this example; but because it happens to illustrate the first fact to be realised about the present position of Cobbett.

In one sense, of course, Cobbett has never been neglected. He has only been admired in the way in which he would have specially hated to be admired. He who was full of his subject has been valued only for his style. He who was so stuffed with matter has been admired for his manner; though not perhaps for his manners. He shouted to the uproarious many, and his voice in a faint whisper has reached the refined few; who delicately applauded a

1

turn of diction or a flight of syntax. But if such applause be rather disconcerting to the demagogue, the real revival of his demagogy would he even more disconcerting to the academic admirer. Now I mean by the revival of Cobbett the revival of the things that Cobbett wished to revive. They were things which until a little while ago nobody imagined there was the slightest chance of reviving; such as liberty, England, the family, the honour of the yeoman, and so on. Many of the learned who, on the occasion above mentioned, were very indulgent to my own eccentric enthusiasm, would even now be a little puzzled if that enthusiasm became something more than an eccentricity. Cobbett had been for them a man who praised an extravagant and impossible England in exact and excellent English. It must seem strange indeed that one who can never hope to write such English can yet hope to see such an England. The critics must feel like cultivated gentlemen who, after long relishing Jeremy Taylor's diction, should abruptly receive an unwelcome invitation to give an exhibition of Holy Dying. They must feel like scholars who should have lingered lovingly all their lives over the lapidary Babylonian jests and vast verbal incantations of the wonderful essay on Urn-Burial; and then have lived to see it sold by the hundred as the popular pamphlet of a bustling modern movement in favour of cremation.

Nevertheless, this classic preservation of Cobbett in an urn, in the form of ashes, has not been quite consistent with itself. Even now it would seem that the ashes were still a little too hot to touch. And I only mentioned my own little effort in academic lecturing because it concerned something that may be repeated here, as relevant to the first essentials of the subject. Many professors have in a merely literary sense recognised Cobbett as a model; but few have modelled themselves upon their model. They were always ready to hope that their pupils would write such good English. But they would have been mildly surprised if any pupil had written such plain English. Yet, as I pointed out on that occasion, the strongest quality of Cobbett as a stylist is in the use he made of a certain kind of language: the sort of use commonly called abuse. It is especially his bad language that is always good. It is precisely the passages that have always been recognised as good style that would now be regarded as bad form. And it is precisely these violent passages that especially bring out not only the best capacities of Cobbett but also the best capacities of English. I was and am therefore ready to repeat what I said in my little lecture, and to repeat it quite seriously, though it was the subject at the time of merely amused comment. I pointed out that in the formation of the noble and beautiful English language, out of so many local elements, nothing had emerged more truly beautiful than the sort of English that has been localised under the name of Billingsgate. I pointed out that English excels in certain angular consonants and abrupt terminations that make it extraordinarily effective for the expression of the fighting spirit and a fierce contempt. How fortunate is the condition of the Englishman who can kick people; and how relatively melancholy that of the Frenchman who can only give them a blow of the foot! If we say that two people fight like cat and dog, the very words seem to have in them a shindy of snaps and screams and scratches. If we say *'comme le chat et le chien,'* we are depressed with the suggestion of comparative peace. French has of course its own depths of resounding power: but not this sort of battering ram of bathos. Now nobody denies that Cobbett and his enemies did fight like cat and dog, but it is precisely his fighting passages that contain some of the finest examples of a style as English as the word dog or the word cat. So far as this goes the point has nothing to do with political or moral sympathy with Cobbett's cause. The beauty of his incessant abuse is a matter of art for art's sake. The pleasure which an educated taste would receive in hearing Cobbett call a duchess an old cat or a bishop a dirty dog is almost onomatopoeic, in its love of a melody all but detached from meaning. In saying this, it might be supposed, I was indeed meeting the purely artistic and academic critic half way, and might well have been welcomed, so to speak, with an embrace of reconciliation. This is indeed the reason why most lovers of English letters have at least kept alive a purely literary tradition of Cobbett. But, as it happened, I added some words which I will also take the liberty of mentioning, because they exactly illustrate the stages of this re-emergence of the great writer's fame from the field of literature to the field of life. 'There is a serious danger that this charm in English literature may be lost. The comparative absence of abuse in social and senatorial life may take away one of the beauties of our beautiful and historic speech. Words like "scamp" and "scoundrel", which have the unique strength of English in them, are likely to grow unfamiliar through lack of use, though certainly not through lack of opportunity for use. It is indeed strange that when public life presents so wide and promising a field for the use of these terms, they should be suffered to drop into desuetude. It seems singular that when the careers of our public men, the character of our commercial triumphs, and the general culture and ethic of the modern world seem so specially to invite and, as it were, to cry aloud for the use of such language, the secret of such language should be in danger of being lost.' Now, when I drew the attention of those authoritative guardians of English literature, responsible for the preservation of the purity of the English language, to this deplorable state of things – to the words that are like weapons rusting on the wall, to the most choice terms of abuse becoming obsolete in face of rich and even bewildering opportunities in the way of public persons to apply them to – when I appealed against this neglect of our noble tongue, I am sorry to say that my appeal was received with heartless laughter and was genially criticised in the newspapers as a joke. It was regarded not only as a piece of mild buffoonery but as a sort of eighteenth-century masquerade; as if I only wished to bring back cudgels and cutlasses along with wigs and three-cornered hats. It was assumed that nobody could possibly seriously hope, or even seriously expect, to hear again the old Billingsgate of the hustings and the election fight. And yet, since those criticisms were written, only a very little time ago, that sort of very Early English has suddenly been heard, if not in journalism, at least in politics. By a strange paradox, even the House of Commons has heard the sound of common speech, not wholly unconnected with common sense. Labour members and young Tories have both been heard talking like men in the street. Mr Jack Jones, by his interruptions, has made himself a judicious patron of this literary revival, this attempt to save the heritage of English culture; and Mr Kirkwood has said things about capitalists of which even Cobbett might be proud.

Now, I have only mentioned my premature lament over the bargee, that disreputable Tom Bowling, because it serves to introduce a certain equally premature rejoicing which explains much of our present position. The Victorian critics had insisted on regarding the violence of Cobbett as entirely a thing of the past; with the result that they find themselves suddenly threatened with that sort of violence advancing on them from the future. They are perhaps a little alarmed; and at least they are very naturally puzzled. They had always been taught that Cobbett was a crank whose theories had been thrashed out long ago and found to be quite empty and fallacious. He had been preserved only for his style; and even that was rude and old-fashioned, especially in the quaint Saxon archaism of calling a spade a spade. They little thought to have heard the horrid sound, the hideous word 'spade' itself shake the arches of St Stephen's as with a blasphemy. But the question is not merely one of idioms but of ideas. They had always supposed at least that Cobbett's ideas were exploded; and they found they were still exploding. They found that the explosion which missed fire a hundred years ago, like that of Guy Fawkes three hundred years ago, still has a time fuse whose time was not quite expired; and that the location of the peril (I regret to say) was also not very far from the same spot as Guy Fawkes'. In a peril of that sort it is very important to understand what is really happening; and I doubt if the comfortable classes understand what is happening much better than they did in Cobbett's day – to say nothing of Guy Fawkes'. And one reason why I originally agreed to write this little book, is that I think it a matter of life and death that it should be understood.

The cudgel has come back like a boomerang: and the common Englishman, so long content with taking half a loaf, may yet in the same tradition of compromise confine himself to heaving half a brick. The reason why Parliamentary language is unparliamentary and Westminster has been joined to Billingsgate, the reason why the English poor in many places are no longer grumbling or even growling but rather howling, the reason why there is a new

4

note in our old polite politics, is a reason that vitally concerns the subject of this little study. There are a great many ways of stating that reason; but the way most relevant here is this. All this is happening because the critics have been all wrong about Cobbett. I mean they were specially wrong about what he represented. It is happening because Cobbett was *not* what they have always represented him as being; not even what they have always praised him as being; it is happening because Cobbett stood for a reality of quite another sort; and realities can return whether we understand them or not. Cobbett was *not* merely a wrong-headed fellow with a knack of saying the right word about the wrong thing. Cobbett was *not* merely an angry and antiquated old farmer who thought the country must be going to the dogs because the whole world was not given up to the cows. Cobbett was not merely a man with a lot of nonsensical notions that could be exploded by political economy; a man looking to turn England into an Eden that should grow nothing but Cobbett's Corn. What he saw was not an Eden that cannot exist but rather an Inferno that can exist, and even that does exist. What he saw was the perishing of the whole English power of self support, the growth of cities that drain and dry up the countryside, the growth of dense dependent populations incapable of finding their own food, the toppling triumph of machines over men, the sprawling omnipotence of financiers over patriots, the herding of humanity in nomadic masses whose very homes are homeless, the terrible necessity of peace and the terrible probability of war, all the loading up of our little island like a sinking ship; the wealth that may mean famine and the culture that may mean despair; the bread of Midas and the sword of Damocles. In a word, he saw what we see, but he saw it when it was not there. And some cannot see it – even when it is there.

It is the paradox of his life that he loved the past, and he alone really lived in the future. That is, he alone lived in the real future. The future was a fog, as it always is; and in some ways his largely instinctive intelligence was foggy enough about it. But he and he alone had some notion of the sort of London fog that it was going to be. He was in France during the French Revolution; amid all that world of carnage and classical quotations, of Greek names and very Latin riots. He must have looked, as he stood there with his big heavy figure and black beaver hat, as solemn and solid a specimen as ever was seen of the Englishman abroad – the sort of Englishman who is very much abroad. He went to America just after the American Revolution; and played the part of the old Tory farmer, waving the beaver hat and calling on those astonished republicans for three cheers for King George. Everywhere, amid all that dance of humanitarian hopes, he seemed like a survival and a relic of times gone by. And he alone was in any living touch with the times that were to come.

All those reformers and revolutionists around him, talking hopefully of the future, were without exception living in the past. The very future they happily prophesied was the future as it would have been in the past. Some were dreaming of a remote and some of a recent past; some of a true and some of a false past; some of a heroic past and others of a past more dubious. But they all meant by their ideal democracy what democracy would have been in a simpler age than their own. The French republicans were living in the lost republics of the Mediterranean; in the cold volcanoes of Athens and Thebes. Theirs was a great ideal; but no modern state is small enough to achieve anything so great. We might say that some of those eighteenth-century progressives had even got so far as the reign of Pepin or Dagobert, and discovered the existence of the French Monarchy. For things so genuine and primarily so popular as the French Monarchy are generally not really discovered until they have existed for some time; and when they are discovered they are generally destroyed. The English and to some extent the American liberals were living in one sense even more in the past; for they were not destroying what had recently been discovered. They were destroying what had recently been destroyed. The Americans were defying George the Third, under the extraordinary idea that George the Third ruled England. When they set up their republic, the simple colonists probably really did think that England was a monarchy. The same illusion filled the English Whigs; but it was only because England had once been a monarchy. The Whigs were engaged permanently in expelling the Stuarts, an enjoyable occupation that could be indefinitely repeated. They were always fighting the battles of Naseby and Newbury over again, and defying a divine right that nobody was defending. For them indeed Charles the First walked and talked half an hour, or half a century, or a century and a half, after his head was cut off; and they themselves could walk nowhere but in Whitehall, and talk of nothing but what happened there. We can see how that long tradition lingered in a light and popular book like Dickens' *Child's History of England*; and how even the child was still summoned to take part in that retrospective revolution. For there were moments when even Mr Dickens had the same obsession as Mr Dick.

But the point is that these idealists – most of them very noble idealists – all saw the future upon the simple pattern of the past. It is typical that the American band of comrades were called the Cincinnati, and were named after Cincinnatus the Consul who threw away the toga to take the plough. But Cobbett knew a little more about ploughing. He knew the ploughshare had stuck in a stiff furrow; and he knew as nobody else knew upon what sort of stone it had struck. He knew that stone was the metal out of which the whole modern world would be made; unless the operation could be stopped in time. He knew it indeed only blindly and instinctively but nobody else knew it at all.

Nobody else had felt the future; nobody else had smelt the fog; nobody else had any notion of what was really coming upon the world.

I mean that if you had gone to Jefferson at the moment when he was writing the Declaration of Independence, and shown him the exact picture of an Oil Trust, and its present position in America, he would have said, 'It is not to be believed.' If you had gone to Cobbett, and shown him the same thing, he would have said, like the bearded old gentleman in the rhyme, 'It is just as I feared.' If you had confronted Carnot with Caillaux, the old revolutionist would have wondered what inconceivable curse could have fallen on great France of the soldiers. If you had confronted Cobbett with some of our similar specimens, he would have said it was what might be expected when you gave over great England to the stockjobbers. For men like Jefferson and Carnot were thinking of an ancient agricultural society merely changing from inequality to equality. They were thinking of Greek and Roman villages in which democracy had driven out oligarchy. They were thinking of a medieval manor that had become a medieval commune. The merchant and man of affairs was a small and harmless by-product of their system; they had no notion that it would grow large enough to swallow all the rest. The point about Cobbett is that he alone really knew that *there* and not in kings or republics, Jacobins or Anti-Jacobins, lay the peril and oppression of the times to come.

It is the riddle of the man that if he was wrong then, he is right now. As a dead man fighting with dead men, he can still very easily be covered with derision; but if we imagine him still alive and talking to living men, his remarks are rather uncomfortably like life. The very words that we should once have read as the most faded and antiquated history can now be read as the most startling and topical journalism. Let it be granted that the denunciation was not always correct about Dr Priestley or Dr Rush; that the abuse was not really applicable to Mr Hunt or Mr Wright; let us console ourselves with the fact that the abuse is quite applicable to us. We at least have done all that Cobbett's enemies were accused of doing. We have fulfilled all those wild prophecies; we have justified all those most unjustifiable aspersions; we have come into the world as if to embody and fulfil in a belated fashion that highly improbable prediction. Cobbett's enemies may or may not have ruined agriculture; but anyhow we have. Cobbett's contemporaries may or may not have decreased the national wealth; but it is decreased. Paper money may not have driven out gold in his lifetime, but we have been more privileged than he. In a mere quarrel between the eighteenth century and the nineteenth century he may easily appear wrong; but in a quarrel between the nineteenth century and the twentieth century he is right. He did not always draw precise diagrams of things as they were. He only had frantic and fantastic nightmares of things as they are. The fame of Cobbett faded and indeed completely vanished during our time of prosperity; or what is counted our time of prosperity. For in fact it was only the prosperity of the prosperous. But during all that time his version of the doubts about what Carlyle called the profit-and-loss philosophy practically disappeared from the modern mind. I have mentioned Carlyle; but as expressed by Carlyle the same doubts were not the same thing. Carlyle would have turned capitalism into a sort of feudalism, with the feudal loyalty on the one side and the feudal liberality on the other. He meant by the profit-and-loss philosophy a small and mean philosophy that could not face a small loss even for the sake of a great profit. But he never denied that there could be a great profit; he never contradicted the whole trend of the age as Cobbett did. On the contrary, Carlyle called the capitalist by a romantic name, where Cobbett would have called him by a shockingly realistic name. Carlyle called the capitalist a captain of industry; a very sad scrap of Victorian sentimentalism. That romantic evasion misses the whole point; the point which Cobbett kept steadily in sight all his life. Militarism would be much less respectable and respected if the captain of a line regiment had pocketed the rent of every acre that he fought for in Flanders. Capitalism would be much more respectable and respected if all the master builders climbed to the tops of towers and fell off; if there were as many capitalists knocked on the head by bricks as there were captains killed at the front by bullets. But as I pointed out in a connection already mentioned, Carlyle was really rather an optimist than a pessimist. Certainly Carlyle was an optimist where Cobbett was a pessimist. Cobbett dug much deeper: he not only called a spade a spade, but he used it like a resurrectionist – not merely like a reformer weeding out small evils. We might say that the mere reformer calls a spade a spud. Carlyle gave hints and suggestions rather darkly that the whole business might end badly; but he never really dared to wish that it had never begun. He told the rich sternly how they should dispose of their wealth; he did not, like Cobbett, tell them coarsely how they had collected it. The consequence was that Carlyle has been exhibited as a Puritan, a pessimist, a prophet of woe. Cobbett has not been exhibited at all. Carlyle has been set over against Mill and Macaulay as a sort of official opposition; but Cobbett's opposition was not sufficiently official. Carlyle has been allowed to grumble like a choleric old major much respected in the club. Cobbett has been entirely removed, like the *enfant terrible*, kicking and screaming, lest he should say something dreadful in the drawing-room. Hence the big secret with which he was bursting has actually been too big to be uttered; his condemnation was so large and sweeping that it had to be hidden in a hole. The Victorians were quite cultivated enough and broad-minded enough to realise that there must be some reminder amid their rejoicings of human fallibility and frailty; lest Mr George Augustus Sala should seem a creature all too bright and good for human nature's daily food. They had something of the imperial imagination and philosophic outlook of the ancient Egyptians, who set a skeleton at the banquet to remind them of mortality and a more melancholy mood that might mingle harmlessly with the mood of joy. Carlyle was the skeleton of the feast. But Cobbett was not the skeleton of the feast; he was the skeleton in the cupboard.

In short, Carlyle did criticise the profit-and-loss school, but not the profitableness of the whole world in which it was made. Certainly he did not question the assumption that it was at least profitable in the sense of being practicable. But since then deeper forces have moved and darker riddles begun to be murmured amongst us; and it is not the superficial abnormalities and accidents but the whole main movement and purpose of the nineteenth century that is brought in question. We have come back to doing what Carlyle never really did, what Cobbett always wanted to do, to make a real reckoning of ultimate loss and profit on the profit-and-loss philosophy. Even in the economic sphere the answer has been looking more and more doubtful. We talk of it as the age of profiteers; but it is a question how long even profiteers will make profits. We talk of it as capitalism; and so it is, in the rather sinister sense of living on capital.

So in some old romance of some old manor-house and manorial family there might come a dark hour in its annals and a dark cloud upon its towers (a thunderstorm thrown in, or the fall of some shield or picture or garden statue or anything necessary to the novelist's taste in doom) and through the darkened halls and corridors the master of the house would pass to some dim disordered library and take down some forbidden or neglected volume, in which are traced strange emblems or figures or maps or charts of hidden things, or forgotten runes and riddles returning only with the end. So the Englishman of the twentieth century is today groping his way back past all the literature of the nineteenth; past all the varied Victorian romances of fashionable progress in Macaulay and fashionable reaction in Carlyle; till he finds far up on a high shelf the old thick, leather-bound volumes, with faded print and the barely decipherable title of 'Cobbett's Register' and taking down the book, amid the gathering storm and the growing darkness, reads this old story.

II

A SELF-MADE MAN

It is now rather more than a century and a half since a small boy of the poorer sort was occupied in scaring rooks where they rose, as they still rise, in black flotillas flecking the great white clouds that roll up against the great ridges of Surrey and the southern shires. Yet further south where the Sussex hills take on an outline at once more opulent and more bare there was repeated a rhyme that might run like a refrain through much of his story.

Bees are bees of Paradise.
Do the work of Jesus Christ,
Do the work that no man can;
God made bees and bees make honey,
God made man and man makes money.
God made man to plough and reap and sow,
And God made little boys to scare away the crow.

And so the little boy in question continued to scare away the crow, in obedience to that providential arrangement.

The little boy was destined to grow up into a tall and vigorous man, who was to travel far and into strange places, into exile and into prison and into Parliament; but his heart never wandered very far from the simple ideals that are summed up in that verse. He was no mere dreamer or more or less lovable loafer, of the sort sometimes associated with the village genius. He would have been as ready as any man of the utilitarian school to admit that men would do well to imitate the industry of bees. Only, those who look at his literary industry may be tempted to say that he had more sting than honey. Similarly he was no mere romantic or sentimentalist, such as is sometimes associated with a love of the rural scene. He would have been as ready as any merchant or trader to face the fact that man, as God has made him, must make money. But he had a vivid sense that the money must be as solid and honest as the corn and fruit for which it stood, that it must be closely in touch with the realities that it represented; and he waged a furious war on all those indirect and sometimes imaginary processes of debts and shares and promises and percentages which make the world of wealth today a world at the worst unreal and at the best unseen. He was most immediately concerned, in the conditions of the hour, with what he regarded as the fugitive and wasteful paper chase of paper money. But what he was at once predicting and denouncing, like a small cloud that had not yet become a universal fog, was that vast legal fiction that we call finance. In any case, against a world in which such financial mysteries were multiplying every day, in which machinery was everywhere on the march, and the new towns spreading with the swiftness of a landslide, in which England was already well on the way to becoming merely the workshop of the world, against the whole great crawling labyrinth of the modern state which is almost one with the modern city, there remained in him unaltered, cut deep into the solitary rock of his soul, the single clause of his single creed: that God made man to plough and reap and sow.

For this was William Cobbett, who was born in 1762 at a little farm at Farnham in Surrey. His grandfather had been an ordinary agricultural labourer, one of a class drudging for a miserable wage, and fallen so far from anything resembling the pride of a peasantry that in English history it had utterly sunk out of sight. It was something that has hardly been known since heathen times; there rests on all its records the ancient silence of slavery. It was to these slaves that the heart of Cobbett continually turned, in what seemed to many its dizzy and incalculable turnings. Those that were trampled and forgotten alike by the Tory squire and the Radical merchant were those whom Cobbett cared to remember; exactly as both Patrician and Plebeian citizens might have been puzzled by a sage whose first thought was of the slaves. And if ever in this land of ours the poor are truly lifted up, if ever the really needy find a tongue for their own needs, if ever progressives and reactionaries alike realise upon what ruins were built both their order and their reform, how many failures went to make their success, and what crimes have set their house in order, if they see the underside of their own history with its secrets of sealed-up wrath and irrevocable injustice – in a word, if a great people can ever repent, then posterity may see achieved by this agency also, by this one lonely and angry bee in whom society saw nothing but a hornet, the work of Jesus Christ.

His father was a small farmer and evidently no fool; but the son could have but a very rudimentary and rustic schooling. The son was perhaps all his life a little too prone to play the schoolmaster; and from an early age he played the schoolmaster to himself. We have many notes of his first reading; notably a glimpse which shows him gaping at the broad farcical title of 'The Tale of a Tub,' so much in his own verbal fashion, and buying it and trying to understand it. He read it under a haystack, and it was so that there fell across him in his first sunshine the shadow of that dark but not ignoble spirit who a hundred years before had seen the first victory of our Venetian oligarchy and despaired. For many have discussed whether Cobbett owed anything to Swift's style, but few have sufficiently considered his connection with Swift's cause or creed. Anyhow, precious little of either could have been made out by a farmer's boy reading 'The Tale of a Tub' under a haystack. For the rest, there is something of the boy's adventure story running through his boyhood. He embodied the recognised romance of England by running away to sea. He also embodied his own rather recurrent and fitful sagacity by running back again.

He was a character from his earliest years. There was a sort of calm impetuosity about his movements. He set out one day to escort some girls to the village fair, dressed up in all his village finery. He saw a coach with 'London' on it, and inconsequently got on to it and went careering away, leaving his lady friends, his fair, his farm, and his family behind him like things of the past. Fortunately he met a friend of his father's in London, who got him a post as clerk in a lawyer's office. He hated the lawyer's office, as he hated lawyers and law all his life; as he hated long words and pedantry and petty tyranny. He took another plunge with the same placid abruptness; he took the King's shilling and enlisted as a private soldier. Here he was more successful; for there was much more of the soldier than the lawyer about him. Moreover, he was none the less a country boy because he had played the traditional part of the country boy who comes up to London where the streets are paved with gold. He was tall and strong, with a stride for which there seemed to be no room in the narrow streets, which went with a better swing on the long marches over the hills and far away. His lungs, which in every sense played so large a part in his life, demanded the deep air of the open places. Fifty years afterwards, at Westminster, as he would have said, he was to find himself dying in another den of lawyers, he was much happier anyhow in the camp of soldiers; indeed, he was not only happy but fortunate. He was recognised as a good soldier, and rose to be corporal and sergeant and eventually a sort of secretary to the whole regiment, assisting the adjutant. All this time he had been teaching himself grammar; and also (what is pleasingly characteristic) teaching the adjutant grammar. Anyhow it is obvious that he was trustworthy and that he was trusted. He was strict in his duty; rose early, an early bird ready to catch the earliest worm; he kept an eye on everything; he was as busy as a businessman. Such a man generally dies rich and respected;

but it is just here that there appears that little twist or bias which decided how William Cobbett was to live and die.

Cobbett began to note something queer and quite wrong about the regimental accounts. He soon discovered that a number of officers were simply pocketing money meant for the regimental food. Then it was that there appeared the deplorable difference between Cobbett and a really respectable and successful man. All his life long he never could leave things alone. He was a businessman: but he could not mind his own business. He kept an eye on things; but he had never learnt to wink the other eye. He was the early bird; but he fell into the melancholy mistake of supposing that all worms ought really to be treated as worms. He had not the fine instinct which makes the really successful secretary-bird distinguish between the earthworms of the underworld and the silkworms of the smart set. It is not suggested that he was a pure altruist, a spotless saint of patriotism; then as always his action involved a vast amount of vanity, of self-assertion, of sensationalism and crudity, also a vast amount of inconsistency and inconsequence. The point is that, whatever his other vices, he did not really know how to rise in the world. He made a scene; and discovered too late that in denouncing what he supposed to be a detail of individual swindling in his own regiment he had really challenged a system running through the whole British Army, or for that matter through the whole British Constitution. Where his restless meddling thought to let the regimental cat out of the bag, or out of one particular knapsack, he found he had roused from its lair a sort of Tammany Tiger. He was not by any means clear or consistent about it. The truth is he was quite out of his depth yet he was perfectly right in feeling that there were depths of degradation. While he was in the Army his protest was easily crushed; when he had left it the Government granted some sort of enquiry; but as Cobbett could not get what he demanded as the conditions of that enquiry, he refused even to attend it himself, and the whole protest went by default. In a society like ours, it is very common for scandals that are too big to be cured to fizzle out like that, as if they were too small to be considered.

It was while he was a soldier that he took another of those characteristic steps, that might seem to many like steps over a precipice. But it is essential to realise about him that the very first step always had about it something almost stiff and automatic in its composure, however stormy might be the consequences or however much he might rave back against the storm. In this connection we must try to remember what is so entirely forgotten: the Stoic ideal of the end of the eighteenth century. The secular ideals of humanity fossilise very fast, and nothing but religion ever remains. Stoicism is stratified amid layers of lost moral fashions; but it was a fine thing in its day, when it stiffened with heathen virtues the Revolutionists of France and America. Our luxurious and orientalised fashions and fictions have a great deal to learn from the Roman virtues advocated in *Sandford and Merton*. That is why they certainly will not learn it. It must be admitted that in Mr Cobbett there was a touch of Mr Barlow. All his life he admired people who did things for themselves; especially if they did them under difficulties. He admired homemade bread or home-brewed ale even if some would call it the bread of affliction or consider it very bitter beer. Very early one morning he was going some of his military rounds in his sergeant's uniform, when the grey day was just breaking over fields of snow. He had a great power of sketching a landscape in simple words; and somehow such a twilight of grey and silver remains long in the reader's memory. At the end of a small yard he saw a girl with dark hair scouring out some pots and pans. He looked at her again and saw she was very beautiful. Then he said with a sort of fatal finality: 'That's the girl for me.' And indeed she was the wife who was with him when he died fifty years afterwards, on those Surrey hills that were his home.

Another incident attaches itself to her memory which is very significant of Cobbett's career from its earliest days. Doubtless he had before and since taken many girls to fairs, or failed to take them to fairs, like those who must have waited wondering after the incident of the coach. But like many combative, objective men he was really by nature very faithful in relations of mere affection; and he makes us believe it by a very convincing account of his one serious temptation to unfaithfulness. Unfaithfulness is never so vivid to an unfaithful man. By the time he returned to England, it was with the perfectly simple and concentrated purpose of seeking out the girl he had seen in the snow. In the old days he had come to a sort of understanding with her; and had solemnly placed in her hands a sealed packet of money, telling her to use it whenever she was in need. Then his regiment crossed the Atlantic and she was lost in the labyrinth of the poverty of a modern town. For a long time he could find no trace; at last he tracked her to a slum where she was working as the poorest sort of servant; and she handed him back his packet of money with the seal unbroken.

It is clear that for Cobbett that small gesture of repayment seemed as splendid as the throwing of the gauntlet. To enter into his sense of triumph we must understand something that is found in him through life, and especially found in him, when it is generally rarest, in youth. It is something seldom understood in a society without peasants; an oligarchy which can only understand what we call 'honour' as it is understood by gentlemen. It was the self-respect of the poor, which all modern industrial society has been slowly crushing to death. To find it anywhere uncrushed and even uncowed was to Cobbett like the noise of a great victory in a war of the world. When the poor servant-girl stood up and handed him back his little handful, there were things in it that neither snobs nor Bohemians will ever understand. There was at once fidelity and defiance, there was at once loyalty and solitude, there was

14

a hard pride in work and a fine shade of delicacy; there was dignity, there was justice, above all there was triumph. Not here at least had the almighty meanness of the modern world prevailed, that lopped all lofty simplicities and lamed all lovers' quests; here was a romance rounded and complete and solid as the sealed packet in his hand; here in this unhappy world was a story with a happy ending. In all the long comedy of the contrast between the heart of man and its surroundings, never has there been a stranger disproportion than between the outside and the inside of that one small incident; of a young man finding his first love left alone with her honour and her pride. To anyone passing in the street there could have been nothing visible but a tall and shabby soldier staring at a servant-girl on a doorstep; but in his own narration it becomes easy to understand that she came back to him with all the beauty of banners.

I have dwelt on this one case of the contrast between the external homeliness of poverty and the internal glow of its occasional festivals and triumphs, because this is something very near to the whole secret of the man's life. It was always of such small tragedies and small triumphs that he was thinking when he talked about the problem of poverty. He differed from many modern social reformers and from most modern philanthropists, in the fact that he was not merely concerned with what is called the welfare of the workers. He was very much concerned for their dignity, their good name, their honour, and even their glory. Any humane man may desire the well-being of his servants, as he may the well-being of his horses or his sheep. But he does not commonly expect a horse to bring back a nosebag, full of oats, to which the conscientious quadruped does not think himself entitled by the terms of the contract. He does not expect a sheep to fire up and take offence, either at being bribed with grass or water, or at being criticised as the black sheep of the flock. He does not expect the sheep to offer to fight the sheep dog, when accused of running away from the wolf. In short, he does not expect horses and sheep to have a sense of honour; but Cobbett, always so eccentric and paradoxical, did really desire peasants and working-men to have a sense of honour. The agony of rage in which so much of his life was passed was due to the consciousness that this popular sense of honour was everywhere being broken down by a cruel and ignoble industrialism. His whole life was a resistance to the degradation of the poor; to their degradation in the literal sense of the loss of a step, of a standing, of a status. There lay on his mind, like a nightmare of machinery crushing and crunching millions of bones, all the detailed destruction of the private property and domestic traditions of destitute families; all the selling up and breaking up of furniture, all the pawning of heirlooms and keepsakes; all that is meant by the awful sacrifice of the wedding-ring. He thought of a thousand stories like the story of the servant-girl: except that these stories did not have a happy ending.

His wife was soon to discover that if she had married (as she had) one of the most constant and considerate of husbands, she had also married one of the most restless and incalculable of men. It would be instructive to have a diary of Mrs Cobbett, as well as the endless autobiographies of Mr Cobbett. But she remains in the background of his life in a sort of powerful silence; and is known to us only by the praises that he never ceased to give her. She was soon called upon to go on some of his interminable travels. When he found in the case of Army corruption, to use one of his own homely sort of figures, that he had bitten off more than he could chew, he retired in disgust to France, and remained there through some of the most thrilling days of the French Revolution. Yet it is typical of him that he took with immense seriousness to the subject of French grammar, as a pendant to his devouring hobby of English grammar. When he set sail again from France it was not for England but for America, where he and his wife remained in exile for seven years. Their travels were not without their tragedies; for his first child died and his second was still-born, and it was not until he was more finally established that a living child rejoiced the most enthusiastic of fathers. But through all these early days we have the same vigilant activity in private things; as in the touching story of his striding up and down all night and driving away the howling dogs that his wife might sleep.

But there is another moral affecting the man and his work and arising in this connection out of an incident like that of his courtship and marriage. From the start we find him standing up sternly and almost priggishly for ideals of thrift and self-control. He might almost have been mistaken for a supporter of Smiles and Self-Help, if it were not for his second phase in raising a riot far more reckless than that of Wilkes and Liberty. But he enormously strengthened his case for Liberty by being the very antithesis of Wilkes. He justified his riot precisely because it could not be mistaken merely for riotous living. No sane person could pretend that Cobbett only sympathised with poverty because he sympathised with profligacy; because he sympathised with improvidence and irresponsibility and imbecile waste. Nobody could say he was merely an idler sympathising with idlers, or a wastrel sympathising with wastrels, or a man who loved ignorance preferring those who were ignorant. He was not even a man like Byron or Burns, whose sincere love of public liberty could be confused with a love of private licence. His case against industrialism was immensely strengthened by the fact that he himself was quite cut out to be the industrious apprentice. When he said that thousands were not only unlucky but unjustly oppressed, he said it with the authority of one who might quite well have been the hundredth lucky man who was the only hope of industrial competition. He who was so obviously a self-educated man might surely have been a self-made man. At least he stood a better chance of it than the thousands who were told to live only for that remote chance. When he said that the chance was worthless he was a reasonable and valid witness; when he said that most men were unfairly equipped for the struggle, he was better equipped than most. It was a much wiser Mr Smiles, himself entirely capable of self-help, who saw that the poor were really and truly helpless. And this second consideration comes back to the same truth as the first. It comes back to the fundamental truth of the modern state. Our commercialism does not punish the vices of the poor, but the virtues of the poor. It hampers the human character at its best and not merely at its worst; and makes impossible even the merits that it vainly recommends. Capitalism has prevented the poor man from saving more than it has prevented him from spending. It has restrained him from respectable marriage more than from casual immorality. It may be that Socialism threatens to destroy domesticity; but it is capitalism that destroys it. This is doubtless what is meant by saying that capitalism is the more practical of the two.

Cobbett was eminently and emphatically a respectable man. He was denounced as a demagogue, he was thrown in prison like a felon, he was all his life in the midst of riot and abuse, he was regarded as the inaugurator of red ruin and the breaking up of laws; but he remained to the last a highly respectable person, in the sense that he valued what are called the respectable virtues. That he was respectable to the last is perhaps less remarkable than that he was respectable from the first; and perhaps especially respectable at the first. That period of youth, which is commonly excused as the irresponsible period, was with him by far the most responsible period. It was during that period that he was improving his mind, limiting his luxuries, schooling himself in simple habits and rising in his military profession. He married the girl whose independence and probity he so much admired: and he was all his life a model husband and father. He was respectable and he might easily have been respected. It is his great virtue that he preferred to be reviled. It is his great glory that having taken the first steps in the successful life as it has been lived by so many successful men, he preferred to make himself a mockery and a cockshy for every worldly wit or comfortable critic to laugh at as a failure for a hundred years. He might have been a self-made man; but he died unfinished, trying to make something better than himself.

Finally, he was by nature a traditionalist and he was by tradition a Tory. He appeared first as a solid and loyal supporter of Church and King; and he appeared with complete success. As we shall see, his place was prepared for him as a good party man; his path was straight before him to the position of a great party leader. It seemed to most honest people, it seemed to him quite honestly, his logical and legitimate goal. It is his glory that he never reached his goal. It is his merit that his fallen figure was found far astray, and picked up, so to speak, like a dead vagabond; a puzzle for pedants and a sort of suicidal wreck to politicians; when he had set out on his journey stiff with so many strict loyalties and so many respectable conventions. For there dwelt within him a divine spirit more restless than a devil; a spirit that could not feed on fictions or sleep at the dictation of any drug; an insomnia of intelligence that could not choose but understand; a lidless eye that could not escape from seeing; a surge of spontaneous protest almost as involuntary as vomiting and stronger than the strength of fear; a voice not to be strangled, which for ever, in a fashion so fierce and unfamiliar that it startled men like the roar of a blind beast, appealed from tyranny to God.

III

THE TRAGEDY OF THE PATRIOT

A book like this can be but a bare outline of a life so full as that of William Cobbett. Nevertheless an outline is needed; and it is an outline that is not often supplied. It is the advantage of such a small scope that it can focus what often seems formless and sprawling, through being too large to be seen. Cobbett produced a vast and voluminous mass of work; and vast and voluminous masses of work have been produced about Cobbett. Most of it is interesting and much of it is true; but none of it is the truth. What is wanted in modern biography is something as simple as the single line that marks the sweeping curve or the sharp corner in a weather-chart; or that yet more simple line that runs round the nose or chin in a caricature. There have been caricatures enough of Cobbett; but they caricatured the wrong features. They missed the point. The subject of Cobbett has been admirably amplified; but when it has been simplified, it has been simplified wrong.

The story of Cobbett was a tragedy; a tragedy of a certain type. It was the disillusionment of a patriot. That definition covers all that is called its bewildering inconsistency. I do not mean to imply that he lost his patriotism. He most certainly retained it; that was the tragedy. But he began by having the ordinary optimistic patriotism that looks outwards, and it changed into a pessimistic patriotism that looked inwards. His earlier and more cheerful attitude was one of mere defiance; but it grew to be a much more gloomy attitude when it seriously passed from defiance to defence. It was like the difference between a man blowing a trumpet and a man examining the condition of a gun. But there was also bound up in it the whole business of the modern economic problem; of the industrial individualism that produced the proletarian peril; in short, the whole problem of modern England. We

19

may say of Cobbett, as of more than one great man, that some of the most important incidents in his life happened after he was dead. But the truth to seize at this stage is the truth about this transition from a sort of centrifugal nationalism, that was cheery and even cheeky, to a sort of centrifugal nationalism that was grave and even grim. A modern writer, resembling Cobbett only in having proved that the highest literary genius can be combined with publicity and popular journalism, has called one of his books of essays *An Englishman Looks at the World*. It would have fitted very well the first essays of Cobbett. But the time came when a deeper, a darker, a more withering experience might have carried the title: *An Englishman Looks at England.*

The first fact about this first phase is that the patriotism of Cobbett was the passionate patriotism of the exile. He went to America while he was still quite young; so that even his memories of England were almost memories of childhood. They had not only the glamour of distance, but the glamour of which Wordsworth wrote, the glory and the freshness of a dream. The islands of the blest were supposed to be to the west like Atlantis; but every man who has really sailed to Atlantis knows that the islands of the blest are left behind. Certainly all the islanders who have ever set forth from these islands to the modern Atlantis are at one in having that homing imagination that wings its way backward into the sunrise. Greatly as they have disagreed among themselves, they all agree in that. Perhaps the one rallying point for all Britons is that their songs in America have been songs of exile. The most familiar of them represents the Irishman with his bundle bound for Philadelphia, or the Englishman whistling 'Falmouth is a fine town' as he walks down the street of Baltimore, or the Scotsman rising to that high note not unworthy of the waters of Babylon,

> But still our hearts are true, our hearts are Highland,
> And we in dreams behold the Hebrides.

So strong is such a tradition that later generations will dream of what they have never seen. The nationalism is most intense where the nation is only a name. The Irish American is more Irish than the Irish. The English colonial loyalist is more loyal than an Englishman. The loves and hatreds harden in that hard air and under those clear skies of the western world. They are unsoftened by all the internal doubts and criticisms that come from being on the spot. But with Cobbett this ignorance of interior details was combined with the memories of one who had from childhood an eye for detail, especially for the detail of fields and skies. He remembered England as a great green nursery; and felt as homesick in America as a boy sent to a big, bare, strange, uncomfortable boarding school.

Nowhere in the world does an Englishman feel so much a stranger as in America. He does not necessarily dislike America; and Cobbett himself came to like it in the long run. He simply feels it is a stranger place than France or Flanders or Italy; that it is really the other side of the world like the other side of the moon. But if an Englishman still feels like this, in spite of the hypnotism of the talk about an Anglo-Saxon race and the hope of an Anglo-American alliance, it was immeasurably more so when Cobbett landed in what had quite recently been enemy territory. He met not only an alien atmosphere but a blast of hatred against England.

There were indeed some Americans who sympathised with England as compared with France. They were those grouped around Hamilton, who being avowedly anti-popular in his politics was not likely to be very popular in his personality. They counted a certain number of New England Puritans; for almost the only real resemblance between New England and Old England was that neither of them could make head or tail of France. But though historians divide American opinion into the French party and the English party, I suspect that the atmosphere of popular sympathy was far more French than English. The whole romance of America consisted of rebellion against England; except that part of it that consisted of rescue by France. Nobody who knows what popular legends are like could expect the princess suddenly to take the side of the dragon against St George. It was quite true, of course, that England was by no means merely a dragon and France was by no means only a saint. But in revolutions strong enough to overthrow all historic authorities and create a new nationality there must be the sort of impatient simplicity that sees characters in black and white; and few men at that moment could persuade a real American mob that England was not so black as she was painted. Moreover, the men of that age did not talk about racial unity; and they were bound to France by something like a religious unity. To leave out the definite democratic creed in judging Jefferson and his contemporaries is exactly like leaving Mohammedanism out of Mahomet. England did not believe in that democratic creed; and, being honest in those days, did not pretend to do so for a moment. I take it that the air that Cobbett had to breathe was not only American but Anti-English.

It is part of the picturesque combat of personalities throughout his life that his first cockshy was, of all men in the world, the famous Priestley, the Unitarian and friend of French or American ideals in England. Priestley was a type of the sort of idealist whose ideals are pure but just a little perverse; the sort of internationalist who is specially unpopular among nationalists. The slight superiority in the tone of such intellectuals towards the popular patriotism of their hour aroused Cobbett to a rage quite ignorant and incongruous and yet not unhealthy. What probably made the refined Unitarian very annoying to the unrefined Surrey farmer was the notion of attacking England in America. For exile affected the Surrey farmer in quite the opposite way. It drove him to representing England as a sort of Eden from which he and Dr Priestley had been driven forth; only that Priestley slandered that paradise and it was left for Cobbett to defend it. In a series of furious pamphlets with the appropriate signature of Peter Porcupine, he not only attacked the English democrats but to a great extent the American democracy. It is important to note that his motive was much more patriotism than conservatism. It is sometimes said that Cobbett began in pure conservatism; men talk of him as a Tory from the start; but even from the start the case was more complex than that. His old father the farmer, if he was a Tory, was a Tory with ideas of his own, for he defended the American rebels and Cobbett had first gone to America bearing a letter to the great Thomas Jefferson. He did not defend England because England was monarchical and he was a Royalist, or because England was aristocratic and he was a snob, or because England was the home of Toryism and he was a Tory. He defended England because England was attacked and he was an Englishman; and his real rage was reserved for other Englishmen who attacked her, or seemed to him not sufficiently to defend her. For this reason he extravagantly abused Dr Priestley, for this reason he extravagantly abused Tom Paine, the author of *The Age of Reason*: writing a bitter burlesque life of that author, full of innocent lies: a story with a strange sequel. For this reason he lectured the wondering people of that western land about the beauty of time British Constitution, of British laws, of British landlords, of British military policy, of almost everything, in fact, that he was afterwards famous for rending and rolling in the mud.

Meanwhile his pamphleteering was getting better and better; those quaint studies of English grammar in the corners of the cold barracks at daybreak had trained him not only in language but in logic; and the furious tenderness of exile gave him inspiration. Towards the end of his American visit he showed his uncontrollable fancy for having a finger in every pie by denouncing an American doctor as a quack. He lost his case and was cast in heavy damages; so that he decided to quit the country, leaving behind him a farewell address to the Americans, one of the least friendly farewells to be found in literature. This last American injustice, as he saw it, finally reconciled him to his own country; and it was in a glow of romantic reaction in favour of everything English that the exile re-entered England. The crisis of his life came between that hour and the hour some seventeen years later when he left it once more.

The Tories of England, waging war against Republicans abroad and Radicals at home, naturally received the great reactionary with a roar of welcome. The most prominent figure in the political group that received him was William Windham. He was a fine specimen of the old English aristocrat; that is, he was a Whig more Tory than the Tories. He was a fine specimen of the cultivated gentleman and dilettante; and therefore he was educated enough to see that the uneducated demagogue was a genuine English man of letters. He and his friends gave Cobbett the practical backing necessary for the founding of the celebrated *Cobbett's Register*. It may be well to remark that *Cobbett's Register* really was Cobbett's. He retained his intellectual independence; he made no party compact with Windham or anybody else: nay, he flatly refused money from his friends in a way almost tartly honourable. But Windham and he were at one with the enthusiasm with which they flung their energies into the defence of Old England against the French Revolution and its American sympathisers. The swing and momentum of his American triumphs carried Cobbett on like a tide, and he may well have felt that he was at time top of his fortunes. It was just about this time that curious things began to happen.

All the time he had wandered on the bare baked prairies under the hard white light of the western skies, he had remembered the high green fields of his father's farm and the clouds and the comfort of the rain. For him even more than for Nelson, and in another sense, there was something united and almost interchangeable in the three terms of England, home, and beauty. But his was no mere landscape painter's but a land-owner's and a land-worker's love; and he pored more and more intently over the practice and detail of the farming he had known in boyhood. As he looked at crops or barns or orchards, it seemed as if the frown on his shrewd square face became first thoughtful and then doubtful. Things were not going well; and bit by bit he began to work out in his own mind a notion of the cause. For instance, it was essential to true farming that the farmer should be secure on his farm. If he was not legally and literally a peasant proprietor, he must at least be rooted like a peasant. At the moment peasants were being rooted out like weeds instead of being rooted like trees. Landlords were refusing to grant the long leases that gave a status to a yeomanry; they were chopping them up into shorter terms, and shifting and evicting for higher rents. And when he looked for the cause of this, he thought he had found it in the new fluctuation of prices and even of the value of money; in the paper money that symbolised to him such insecurity and shuffling and sharp practice. It meant the destruction not only of the old sort of yeoman but of the old sort of squire. Stockbrokers and Jews and jobbers from the town were driving out the national gentry; he would appeal to the great leaders of the party of the gentry to save them. He turned to his own Tory leaders, to Windham and the party of Pitt; for they were the natural saviours of the green countryside from this yellow fever of finance.

There is sometimes in a great comedy a scene of almost tragic irony, when some simple character enters, eager, voluble, and full of his subject, and pours it out quite confidently to a group of listeners. It is long before even the spectator realises that the listeners are very silent. It is much longer before the speaker realises it. It is long before even a hint leads him to look, at first with doubt and at last with horror, at the significant and sinister smile faintly present on all those unanswering faces. That was the sort of scene that occurred in history when Cobbett came rushing to his Tory friends with his great scheme for saving English agriculture. He did not understand that restrained smirk on the pinched face of Pitt; that shadow of something like shame that may have rested for a moment on the more generous face of Windham. We could imagine one of them looking at the ceiling and the other at the floor; and neither answering a word.

For William Cobbett had not in fact the faintest notion of what manner of men he served, or what sort of Government he was supporting. If Cobbett eventually found that the Tories were not satisfactory, it was for the very simple reason that he found that the Tories were not Tories. They may have had a desire to restore the old regime in France, largely because it would mean France being less vigorous and victorious than under the new regime of Napoleon. But they had not the faintest desire to save the old regime in England. Why should they? Men like Pitt and Perceval and the rest were more entangled with the new world than ever they were with the old; and were in much closer touch with the stockbrokers than with the farmers. Above all they had no notion of what Cobbett was talking about when he talked of giving the farmer the stability of a yeoman. The only laws they could imagine as applicable to rural life were the game laws. For that purpose perhaps it was desirable that the country should continue to exist. It was seldom possible to start a hare in Lombard Street, and quite awkward to shoot a partridge in Threadneedle Street. Otherwise there was really no reason why Lombard Street and Threadneedle Street should not extend to the ends of the earth. The educated class in England knew much more about preserving pheasants than peasants: it was an aitch they were very careful not to drop.

The biographies of Cobbett commonly say that he began life as a Tory and afterwards changed his politics and became a sort of Radical. The proportions of this picture are misleading. Cobbett was never anything that an enemy would call a turncoat or a friend would call a brand from the burning. There is no sharp break in his life, breaking the very backbone of his principles, such as there is in the life of a penitent or the life of a traitor. It is not true that he belonged successively to two parties: it is much truer to say that he never belonged to any. But in so far as there were elements of the Radical in him at the end, there had been traces of them from the beginning. And in so far as he was in one sense a Tory at the beginning, he remained a Tory to the end. The truth is that the confusion was not in Cobbett but in the terms Tory and Radical. They are not exact terms; they are nothing like so exact as Cobbett was. His general position is intrinsically quite clear and, as men go, quite consistent. It was the Tories who were not clear about Toryism. It was the Radicals who were inconsistent about Radicalism. I do not mean that he had no inconsistencies; he had a great many. He had all those inconsistencies of mere verbal variation which are almost invariable in a man who throws himself with equal vehemence into the proving of many different propositions in many different connections. But the inconsistencies of Cobbett were very superficial; much more superficial than the changes in most political careers. The man who played Peter Porcupine in America did not differ so much from the man who brought the bones of Tom Paine like holy relics to England as the Disraeli of the Revolutionary Epick differed from the Disraeli of the Primrose League, or the Gladstone who was the hope of the stern and unbending Tories from the Gladstone who was the idol of the Radicals and Nonconformists.

Cobbett was a very consistent man, in every essential sense. It was the parties claiming or repudiating him who were quite inconsistent. To understand the point it is necessary to refer briefly to the history of those parties. There had once been something like a real war between Whigs and Tories. It was the real war between aristocracy and monarchy; two mortal enemies who have wrestled through all history. But in England aristocracy had won. Formal histories tell us that the Crown passed from the House of Stuart to the House of Brunswick. But in fact, while the Stuarts lost it, the Brunswicks never got it. The old original Crown the Stuarts had worn was thrown away with the Great Seal, when James the Second fled to France. The young George the Third had indeed tried to recover it with the aid of a Scottish Tory; just as the young Charles Edward had tried to recover it with the aid of the Scottish Jacobites. But it never was recovered. A loyalty to it lingered in middle-class and especially literary circles; as in Johnson and Goldsmith and many of the wisest and best individual thinkers of the eighteenth century. Cobbett came a little too late in time and a little too low in the social scale to touch this old and intelligent Tory middle-class before it died out. I do not know whether he realised how often he visited the Deserted Village in the course of the Rural Rides. Johnson he regarded with one of those accidental animosities that justified to some extent his reputation for mere spite. Cobbett had a prejudice against Johnson; which is all the more amusing because it was exactly the sort of prejudice that Johnson might have had against him. Cobbett regarded Johnson as a mere pedantic pensioner; and Johnson would very possibly have regarded Cobbett as he regarded Wilkes, more or less in the abstract as a dirty demagogue. So many things united these two great Englishmen, and not least their instinctive embodiment of England; they were alike in their benevolent bullying, in something private and practical, and very much to the point in their individual tenderness, in their surly sympathy for the Catholic tradition, in their dark doubts of the coming time. But above all they were united by the thing that divided them: the most genial and humane of all forms of hatred; their passionate and personal hatred of people they had never seen.

In any case, Cobbett was born long after the true Tory monarchy had died, and he never quite understood its tradition. If he grew up a Tory and in some sense remained a Tory, it was in somewhat vaguer traditions that he was traditional. He liked old customs and the continuity of family life to be found in the countryside; he loved England in a sense that was very real and unfortunately very rare. I mean that it was a positive love that looked inwards upon the beloved; and not merely a negative love that looked outwards for rivals or remote imitations. If this sort of love of what is national and normal be called conservative, certainly that character was rooted in him. But what was called his Radicalism was equally radical. He realised by the light of nature the last deductions of time democratic speculators in so far as they can fairly be deduced. But the last conclusions which the republicans could reach were only the ancient axioms on which the monarchies had originally been founded. They were only forgotten because they were fundamental. Cobbett had a great faculty of not forgetting the foundations, as most of us do forget the foundations of a house, especially if we walk about on the roof. He had one very virile sort of simplicity: he was true to the truisms. He was never ashamed of the homely appearance of a humble and a faithful truth. Cobbett always really believed in popular principles, though he saw no cause to talk Greek and call them democratic principles. He could not see that the new industrial progress had anything to do with these principles; and he was perfectly right. He knew that the real revolutionary song had been about fields and furrows, and not about wheels and rails. He knew that the Revolution had begun with bread. He was not in the least impressed by its ending in smoke. The man who had once been a rioter waving the red flag in a revolution may now be a guard waving the red flag on a railway line. But this will not convince the realistic reformer that a railway line is the same as a revolution.

When Radicalism was caught up in the wheel that was the symbol of industrialism, the opposite school tended the opposite way, by the slight movement that makes the balance of a party system. The Tories could pose as the agricultural party; if only a party of squires and not of peasants. But it was no longer a real war, like the war between Parliament and the King, in which Parliament had finally triumphed. The new Whigs and Tories were only two different shades of the same colour, like the dark blue of the Tory University and the light blue of the Whig University. They were at most only two different types of the same oligarchy. They were often only two different generations of the same oligarchy. The one was still making money in the town, while the other had made enough money to live in the country. That Cobbett cut across this sort of distinction of mere sentiment and association is not a mark of his inconsistency but of his consistency. He knew what he wanted; and the Whigs and Tories only offered two slightly different reasons for not giving it to him. There was no logic in the things that held them apart, or in the things they lumped together. There was nothing in the nature of a rational sequence in the notion of one party, standing for aristocracy and the land, and the other for democracy and machinery. It was as meaningless as if one party were associated with justice and beef, while the other was wholly dedicated to mercy and mutton. And it was as if they had joined in reviling the inconsistency of a common-sense person, who desired the more merciful treatment of oxen or the more just distribution of mutton-chops. Now this is why it is vital at this point to realise the true nature of the Tory regime which extends intermittently from Pitt to Peel. Friends and foes alike have treated it as a reactionary regime; but that is only because the facts about it have not been faced. Pitt and his followers were not in the least Tory in the sense of traditional. They were only Tory in the sense of tyrannical. If trying to destroy all old constitutional liberties makes a man a conservative, then certainly Pitt and Castlereagh were model conservatives. But it would be hard to say what it was they conserved. There was not a single historic tradition, not a single human memory of the past, for which they ever showed the faintest sympathy. The truth is that the whole of this passage in history will be read wildly wrong unless we clearly understand that Pitt and Peel were highly modern and purely mercantile figures, helping to found the purely modern and mercantile world. Thus it was Pitt who began time degradation and destruction of a genuine gentry, by selling peerages right and left to every pawnbroker or pork butcher who would pay for them. If ever men were responsible for handing the country over to cads, it was the party of gentlemen who waved the Union Jack after Waterloo. It was so in all the more decent or defensible aspects of commercialism. In that sense Pitt cared nothing for the opinion of the Country Party; or even for the opinion of the Country. What he cared for was the opinion of the City. His real bodyguard was a battalion of bankers. It has often been pointed out that he had many of the merits of a liberal; he had also the vices of a liberal, and especially the liberalities of a liberal. Pitt was the real founder of the Manchester School. Peel only followed the real policy of his party in eventually helping its triumph. We talk of Peel's abrupt acceptance of Free Trade; but it would be truer to talk of his temporary acceptance of Protection. As a type of human being, he had always been purely commercial, and not in the least conservative. In a word, these men did indeed fight democracy abroad and persecute it at home. But they did not defend aristocracy, far less monarchy. What they did was to establish plutocracy; and mainly a parvenu plutocracy. And if it be a glory to have created the modern industrial state, they can claim a very great share in it. Cobbett did not grudge it to them.

Broadly speaking, if there was one man who was bound to be the antithesis of William Cobbett it was William Pitt. Anybody who expected anything else, merely because the two men were at one time classed as Tories, is the person really incapable of understanding intellectual consistency. Cobbett had only supported Pitt because he thought the Pitt rule stood for Old England; but it did not. Cobbett never supported the Pitt party after he had discovered that it did not. It is true that as he drifted further from Pitt and the Tories he necessarily appeared to be drifting nearer to Brougham and the Radicals, who also did not. But the slightest acquaintance with what he said about Brougham and the Radicals will show that it was almost always a movement of repulsion and not of attraction. His preference for any party was rather too comparative to be complimentary. It would hardly have been flattering to Mr Pitt to be told that his appearance had only seemed to be something of a relief after that of Dr Rush, or to Lord Brougham to say that his society seemed quite tolerable to one fleeing from that of Lord Castlereagh. But Cobbett's public alliances, as distinct from his private affections, seldom went much further than this. He may have come eventually almost to hate Orator Hunt; but I doubt whether he had ever really liked him. Windham I am inclined to think that he really liked; and he made earnest efforts to explain to that perplexed Tory that there was nothing inconsistent with Toryism in his pleas for labour and the land. He remained in this doubtful and negative attitude, nearer to the Radicals rather than more Radical, when something happened that changed everything something that broke his life in two in the middle like a blow that breaks the backbone.

He inserted in his *Register* an indignant protest against the flogging of certain English soldiers under a guard of German mercenaries. It is essential to realise that the accent is on the word English and the word German. He was not merely a humanitarian protesting against inhumanity. He was a patriot protesting against his countrymen being tortured to make a spectacle for foreigners. Being a very genuine Englishman, he cared nothing for all the nonsense about allies and enemies, in comparison with the real difference between Englishmen and foreigners. Indeed, by the whole trend of his mind he would always have preferred the French to the German; and nobody would have rejoiced more than he at that great and just alliance that brought about the downfall of Prussia. Anyhow he printed his protest; and instantly discovered that he had touched the spring which launched a whole huge engine of destruction against himself. The great Tory Government, which he had come back from America to serve, had no doubt about how it should deal with this sort of patriotic service. He was instantly pinned with a prosecution, tried before the usual packed jury of the White Terror, and eventually sentenced to imprisonment for two years in Newgate, accompanied by a fine that meant ruin.

Cobbett was bewildered by the blow; and seems at first to have been reduced to despair. It is said that he talked of throwing up his whole public work, since it could not be conducted without involving his family in such ruin. There has been much dispute about the story of some such despairing surrender being communicated to the Government. It seems to me that Cobbett's own account of the incident is probably true in the main; all the more as he owned frankly that his family had once persuaded him to this course: of which, he said, he had afterwards repented. There was some talk of a letter that he had recalled being maliciously published. It is possible: but the whole story seems rather confused. Certainly Cobbett has fought through all his life with weapons of a peculiar baseness; a certain mean spirit which is rather peculiar to such aristocracies when alarmed. It was that mean spirit that stole and published the scandalous poem of Wilkes. It was that spirit which used for political ends the private fault of Parnell. Cobbett suffered from this often enough; but his complaints in this case are rather chaotic and inconsistent. It is very characteristic of Cobbett that even in repudiating the action he argued in defence of it; pointing out that there would be nothing immoral in a private man out of private affection abandoning public work that nobody could demand of him as a duty. His argument was sound enough; but it did not give a real picture of his complex and confused situation. In order to understand the meaning of the whole business, we must understand two things that are relevant to the whole of his life; through the first refers more particularly to this earlier passage in his life. It will be well to get these conceptions clear before this chapter concludes.

First, it must be clearly understood that Cobbett was not yet a Revolutionist; even if he was already a Radical. He was still subconsciously the Tory patriot who had made his name by waging war on all Revolutionists. He had indeed kept his English journalism independent of parties; but if he had originally had any party, it was the Tory party. In other words, his disappointment had begun, but he still had enough admiration to be disappointed. He was still sufficiently orthodox to be troubled by doubt. Then came the shameful and incredible shock of the Constitution he had once defended swinging round and knocking him silly. It was no wonder if, for the moment, it did knock him very silly. But it is reading the last lucid rage of the Radical Cobbett into the first dark and confused doubts of the Conservative Cobbett to expect him to have met his first trial in 1810 as he met his second trial in 1881. His real revolutionary spirit was not the cause of his imprisonment; it was the result of it.

The fools who put Cobbett in prison probably did believe they were crushing a Jacobin, when they were really creating one. And they were creating a Jacobin out of the best Anti-Jacobin of the age. Apart from all

29

political labels, they were manufacturing the greatest rebel of English history out of the most unpromising materials. Perhaps he was the only real rebel that was ever manufactured out of purely English materials. But he was all the more a furious rebel because he was a reluctant rebel. For the man who paced that cell, like a lion in a cage, had not any of the detachment given either by idealism or cynicism. He had not fully learned to expect injustice; he had not yet survived disappointment, the dark surprise of youth. The man in that cell was no Stoic, trained in the Latin logic of Condorcet or Carnot, seeing his own virtues as part of the ideal system of the Republic and his own sufferings as part of the inevitable system of the Kings. He was no Irish martyr, schooled to breathe the very air of tragedy and tyranny and vengeance, and living in a noble but unnatural exaltation of wholly spiritual hate. Like most men of a very English type, he was inordinately fond of happiness. And happiness to him was concrete and not abstract; it was his own farm, his own family, his own children. Like most men of a very masculine type, he was probably a good deal dominated by his wife. And his wife and family had evidently hung on heavily to drag him back from his political precipice. But the worst of it was that he was suffering for an idea; and as yet did not quite know what idea. That is where this great angry and bewildered Englishman differed from the French Stoics or the Irish patriots. They appealed to the gods against the kings, to the ideas against the facts; but it seemed to the Englishman that his own god and king had condemned him. They saw clear skies above a confused world; but it was upon him that his own sky had fallen. He had indeed in his mind all that volcanic amalgam of ancient loyalties and popular sympathies which puzzles the student of party labels; but it was still in his subconscious mind. He had not yet a creed as Robespierre or Jefferson or O'Connell had a creed. In fact, he was not suffering for an idea; he was suffering for an instinct. But the instinct seemed to him a natural part of that natural order which had suddenly sprung on him an unnatural revenge. In so far as he had originally believed in anything, it was in the authorities that had thrown him into gaol. In so far as he had any creed, it had been the Constitution which condemned him as a felon. He had acted on a patriotic impulse; and patriotism had punished him for being patriotic. All this first transition of bewilderment must be allowed for; but when it is allowed for, something else remains. Even when his head had cleared and his creed consolidated, there remained something about him for which the reader must be prepared to make allowances; as much as when we see him swaying rather blindly under this first blow.

Cobbett was a particular human type; the very last to be fairly understood in those quiet times of which the virtue is sociability and the vice is snobbery. He was the imperfect martyr. The modern and popular way of putting it is to say that a man can really be a martyr without being by any means a saint. The more subtle truth is that he can even be a saint and still have that sort of imperfection. The first of Christian saints was in that sense a very imperfect martyr. He eventually suffered martyrdom for a Master whom he had cursed and denied. That marks the tremendous realism of our religion: its heroes had not heroic faults. They had not those Byronic vices that can pose almost as virtues. When they said they were miserable sinners, it was because they really dared to confess the miserable sins. Tradition says that the saint in question actually asked to be crucified upside-down, as if making himself a mere parody of a martyr. And there is something of the same sacred topsy-turvydom in the strange fancy by which he is haunted in all hagiological art and legend by the symbol of his failure. The crowing of a cock, which has become a phrase for insolence, has in this case actually become an emblem of meekness. Rome has lifted up the cock of Peter higher than the eagle of Caesar, not to preach pride to kings but to preach humility to pontiffs. The cock is crowing forever that the saint may never crow.

Cobbett was a much more imperfect martyr; for he lived and died by a much more imperfect light. But this is the contradiction that explains all his contradictions. His courage was not consistent, complete, a thing working itself out by a perfectly clear principle. His heroic stature was not properly or perfectly proportioned; it was merely heroic. He sometimes fell below himself; but it was because he had a far higher and more arduous standard of manhood than most men, especially the men around him. He began tasks that he did not always finish; he took up rash positions that he sometimes found to be untenable. More than once in his career there comes in an element of anticlimax and bathos, at which the world will find it easy to laugh. But the world will have no sort of right to laugh. In the lives of most of us there is no such anticlimax simply because there is no climax. If we do not abandon those tasks it is because we do not attempt them; and we are not crucified upside-down because we have no intention of being crucified at all. The ordinary Sophist or Sadducee, passing the grotesque crucifixion, would have no right to mock the martyr with the crowing of the cock. The ordinary politician or political writer of Cobbett's time or ours had no right to mock the inconsistencies of Cobbett. The whole scheme and standard of his life was higher and harder than theirs, even of the best of them. Men like Bentham and Brougham were sincere reformers in the ordinary sense. Men like Macaulay and Mackintosh were good men in the normal fashion. But they served their world; they never set out to fight the whole world as Cobbett did. Good and bad alike, they are like civilians sitting at home and criticising a shattered and shell-shocked soldier. There is no particular disgrace in being a civilian; though there may be in being an ungenerous civilian.

One example may illustrate what is meant by the comparison. Cobbett got himself flung into a common gaol for protesting against the flogging of

British soldiers in the middle of the Napoleonic war; he afterwards went to America to avoid being flung into prison again. Macaulay, nearly a generation later, in time of peace, when the general mood was much more humanitarian, had the ordinary official task of apologising for flagrantly savage floggings of the same sort, simply because he happened to be Secretary for War and the blustering Lord Cardigan happened to be Commander of the Forces in London. Nobody in his senses would call Macaulay a cruel man. He simply regarded himself as a good party man, making the best of a bad case, as a part of his least agreeable parliamentary duties. His biographer, Sir George Trevelyan, certainly a very liberal and humane man, expresses no particular surprise at it; and nobody felt any particular surprise at it. Most people probably regarded it as we regard the uncomfortable duty of a barrister, who has to minimise the acts of a monster who has tortured children. It was part of the routine, of the rules of the game, of the way of the world. But the man who accepts everything and defends such things is not in the same world with the man who risks everything, or even anything, to denounce them. We may well say about Macaulay what he himself said about Cranmer: 'It is no great condemnation of a man to say that he did not possess heroic fortitude.' And it is no great condemnation of him to say that he will never come within a thousand miles of the man who does possess heroic fortitude, even for a moment.

For if the common or conventional man is not to be condemned for failing to be a hero, still less is the other man to be condemned for succeeding in being half a hero or nine-tenths of a hero. The imperfect martyr may be judged by the perfect martyr, but not by anybody else; and the perfect martyr will probably have the charity as well as the patience of the perfect saint. Nobody will pretend that Cobbett had the patience of the perfect saint. He had not enough of the charity, though he had more than many might suppose, especially the people who make a point of being charitable to the rich. It is true that even his heroism was incalculable and inconsequent; but the question of proportion and even of quantity does not touch the question of quality. One moment of Cobbett's courage is of a different quality from a lifetime of Macaulay's common sense. Macaulay, in his life as in his logic, was nothing worse than superficial. It was the tragedy of Cobbett that he was fundamental. Of all our social critics he was by far the most fundamental. He could not help seeing a fight of first principles deadly enough to daunt any fighter. He could not help realising an evil too large for most men to realise, let alone resist. It was as if he had been given an appalling vision, in which the whole land he looked at, dotted with peaceful houses and indifferent men, had the lines and slopes of a slow earthquake.

Macaulay, it has been noted, said about Cranmer that he could not be blamed for not being a hero and a martyr. But for all that Macaulay blamed him a good deal for being a coward and a snob. Cobbett said about Cranmer that the very thought that such a being had walked the earth on two legs was enough to make the reeling brain doubt the existence of God; but that peace and faith flow back again into the soul when we remember that he was burned alive. I quote the sentiment from memory; but that was the substance of the remark. It is a remark touched with a certain exaggeration. It is not an observation marked primarily by measure or precise proportion or the mellowing of truth with charity. Macaulay's criticism of Cranmer is more effective for everyday purposes; as when he says that the crime of the Tudor politician was not in being too indifferent to be killed, but in killing other people for things about which he was indifferent, and enacting laws against anyone 'who should do from conviction what he had done from cowardice.' But there is a quality in that outburst of Cobbett about Cranmer which we must learn to appreciate or leave off troubling about Cobbett. There is a volume and a violence of humanity in such hatred; a hatred straight from the heart like a knockout blow straight from the shoulder. It is a blast from a furnace. And it is only in such a furnace seven times heated that men suffer for an idea – or even suffer for an impulse.

Anyhow, the only effect of the imprisonment was to turn an impulse into an idea. He may have lacked some of the virtues of a philosopher; even including the philosophy. He may not have been perfect as a hero; or even have possessed any of the qualities of a martyr except the martyrdom. But he was emphatically the sort of man with whom one cannot afford to be in the wrong. It was suicidally silly to act with such injustice to a man with such a talent for expounding justice, including intellectual justice. It would have been wiser in the governing class to have gone on their natural course and continued to harry the imbecile and to torment the dumb. Thousands of poor men have been and are persecuted quite as unjustly as Cobbett by the police and plutocracy of modern states; but a certain political instinct and practical intuition have generally and wisely guided the authorities to hit the sort of man who cannot possibly hit them back. It is impossible not to comment on the very curious carelessness, which in this case allowed the rich and the rulers to commit the customary cruelties upon a man eminently capable of telling the tale. They threw him into gaol for nothing, or for anything, or for something more or less meritorious, for all the world as if he had been his own grandfather the agricultural labourer.

Certainly if they put him in prison, they ought never to have let him out. Surely the flexible British Constitution of Pitt and Castlereagh would have been equal to the necessity of sending him to Botany Bay for life. For that Constitution was very free when it came to attacking freedom. The man who came out of that prison was not the man who went in. It is not enough to say that he came out in a rage, and may be said to have remained in a rage; to have lived in a rage for thirty years, until he died in a rage in his own place upon the hills of Surrey. There are rages and rages; and they ought to have seen in his eyes when they opened the door that they had let loose a revolution. We talk of a man being in a towering passion; and that vigorous English phrase, so much in his own literary manner, is symbolic of his intellectual importance. He did indeed return in a towering passion, a passion that towered above towns and villages like a waterspout, or a cyclone visible from ten counties and crossing England like the stride of the storm. The most terrible of human tongues was loosened and went through the country like a wandering bell, of incessant anger and alarum; till men must have wondered why, when it was in their power, they had not cut it out.

IV

REVOLUTION AND THE BONES OF PAINE

His imprisonment destroyed in Cobbett the whole dream with which he had returned rejoicing from America. That is, it did not in the least destroy his love of his native land; but it did destroy the illusion that he would there be able to breathe quite easily a native air. He could no longer hope, as it had once seemed so natural to do, that the spontaneous and colloquial language that sprang so easily to his own lips would commend itself as easily to people in his own land; that there he would be among neighbours and would talk without an interpreter. England was not a place where they understood plain English. From the very beginning of his fresh start after imprisonment we find him, therefore, facing the fact that he will never be able to say all that he wants to say or to fulfil himself as he had meant to do. Moreover, his fresh start was one not only after imprisonment, but after ruin and practical bankruptcy; and the fresh start was not a very fortunate start. His farming was not successful; his financial difficulties became acute; and it looked as if Cobbett in England would be in every sense a failure. Hence we have to record (before coming to the crowning and decisive part of his English career) another interruption in the form of a visit to America. The visit was a shorter one; and is chiefly interesting through two or three episodes which must be taken in their turn. But we must first say a word of the conditions in his own country.

The first note of the new Cobbett who came out from captivity is the abrupt and absolute cessation of his first boyish feelings about the war with France; the feelings he probably had when he ran away to sea as a boy. He was no longer jolly enough to be a Jingo. I do not use the word in a bad sense; for indeed Cobbett's Jingoism has never been bad enough to be called Imperialism. He had been for fighting the French on the perfectly healthy ground that he was saving his own beloved island from the French. But anyhow this simple way of looking at it became impossible after his imprisonment. He was still a patriot; he was never anything in the least like a pacifist; but he had learnt something that he could not unlearn. He who had cheered on the dogs of war with Windham for a fellow-huntsman called them off abruptly, with a sort of harsh humanitarianism. He came out positively on the side of stopping the war. That is the change that is really significant. He would waste no more time on saving England from the French. He had the huge task of saving England from the English.

Even here, however, it is easy to miss the consistency under all the inconsistencies. It is highly characteristic of him that he had refused with especial fury the proposal to stop the war at an earlier stage, when the proposal was based on the argument (still so common among commercial peacemongers) that war is bad for commerce. Cobbett was quite consistent in having an equal contempt for the Pacifist who made peace for that reason and for the Pittite who made war for that reason. But he was more and more convinced that the Pittites were only making war for that reason. The moment he concluded that only the bankers and merchants really wanted war, and the populace suffered from it without need, he was perfectly consistent in changing sides. He would have been quite inconsistent if he had not changed sides. Windham himself had said, 'Perish Commerce; but let the Constitution be saved.' Cobbett had made it his motto, though now perhaps in the amended form, 'Perish Commerce and Constitutions; but let the country be saved.' Only, he was more and more grimly convinced that it needed saving, and not from Napoleon. He was not less of an English patriot, but perhaps he was in one sense a little less of an Englishman; if being an Englishman means being happy and happy-go-lucky and comforted by compromises and ready to believe anything printed in *The Times*.

Meanwhile the war ended with Waterloo and the peace began with Peterloo. That was the only kind of peace that seemed likely to begin. It was time that somebody did something, whether or no Cobbett could do anything. The new capitalistic phase of England was coming to a crisis, especially in the North. The industrial revolution was already producing the anti-industrial revolution – which is likely to be a much more real revolution. Machines were busy and men were idle. Some men indeed were not idle; but those who were most busy were the political economists, who were busy proving on paper that the machinery that had made people poor must really have made them rich. Very soon something began to happen that anybody might have foreseen, whether he was on the side of the machines or the men, so long as he understood that men are not machines. Cobbett realised it, though he did not approve of it. The men began to destroy the machines; to destroy them as if they were dragons that had come in to destroy the paradise of innocence and liberty. Cobbett, who upon that matter was a moderate, wrote a *Letter to the Luddites*, urging them to desist from this method of protest; but he banded himself with the most resolute of the Radicals, with old Cartwright and Orator Hunt and Burdett, in demanding drastic democratic reforms. His *Register*, already popular at a shilling, was made enormously more popular by being sold for twopence, with the ironic boast of *Twopenny Trash*. Never in English history perhaps has one man wielded so vast and potent a popular instrument as Cobbett did. He and his friends were incessant in demanding reform, which had already begun to be spelt with a capital letter. They pointed to the dark sphinx of industrial destitution and demanded that there should be at least some answer to its riddle.

The answer of the Government was interesting. It was to discover a Plot of the most vast and sanguinary sort started by a Mr Spence, a little bookseller holding the mild sort of Socialism that is called Land Nationalisation. It was called Spencean Philanthropy. All the other reformers were apparently in the plot, however remote or contrary were their notions of reform. Cobbett was about as unlike a Spencean Philanthropist, or indeed any other philanthropist, as any one could conceivably be, but he was supposed to be deep in the plot. The Government hastily armed itself with abnormal powers of violence and secrecy, and threw an iron net of spies and special agents over the whole country to catch all fish, great and small, all reformers, reasonable and unreasonable. One of the big fish decided to break the net before it closed and to get away into other waters. He may have been wise or foolish, but he was in the habit of acting very promptly on his wisdom or folly. Cobbett resolved once more to escape to America and conduct his campaign from there. As a matter of fact, he only stayed there two years, bombarding England with pamphlets all the time, and then came back to follow up his pamphlets with a yet more furious personal onslaught. But he was blamed for his expedient; and indeed it was his fate to go through life being blamed first for attacking and then for retreating, blamed for all he did and all he did not do. Anyhow he thought he was more useful to the reform in America than in gaol; and certainly we should otherwise have lost some protests that were much needed. Nobody else could have done justice to an even more absurd plot called 'the Derbyshire Insurrection,' which was entirely created by an *agent provocateur* named Oliver. It is typical of the wrangles that go on among reformers that if some of the other Radicals blamed Cobbett for escaping to America, he was even more withering about them for playing the coward in England. He denounced them for doing nothing to save the wretched men who suffered from this hideous plot to manufacture a plot. It was on this occasion that Cobbett quarrelled with Burdett, as he afterwards quarrelled with Hunt, and indeed with nearly everybody else. Before leaving for America, indeed, he had had quarrels of less public but more personal importance with his own agents. As already noted, his own economic position was not promising; and this probably contributed to his deciding on a second American visit. In any case, he reached America in the May of 1817, and soon established himself on a farm in Long Island.

Cobbett's second visit to America is associated with an action which all the authorities have censured as ridiculous, and which I think has been ridiculously censured. I do not mean that there was nothing to criticise, but only that there is something quite wrong in the criticisms. The story thus strangely misunderstood is the story of Cobbett carrying back the remains of Thomas Paine, the English Jacobin, to be laid to rest in England.

Thomas Paine invented the name of the Age of Reason; and he was one of those sincere but curiously simple men who really did think that the age of reason was beginning, at about the time when it was really ending. Being a secularist of the most simple-minded sort, he naturally aroused angry passions at the moment, as does any poor fellow who stands on a chair and tries to heckle heaven in Hyde Park. But considering him in retrospect, the modern world will be more disposed to wonder at his belief than at his unbelief. The denial of Christianity is as old as Christianity; we might well say older. The anti-clerical will probably last as long as the Church, which will last as long as the world. But it is doubtful when we shall see again the positive side of Paine's philosophy; the part that was at once credulous and creative. It is impossible, alas, for us to believe that a Republic will put everything right, that elections everywhere will ensure equality for all. For him the Church was at best a beautiful dream and the Republic a human reality; today it is his Republic that is the beautiful dream. There was in that liberalism much of the leisure of the eighteenth-century aristocrats who invented it; and much of the sheltered seclusion also. The garden which Voltaire told a man to cultivate was really almost as innocent as the garden of Eden. But the young men who saw such visions were none the less seeing visions of paradise, though it was an earthly paradise. Rationalism is a romance of youth. There is nothing very much the matter with the age of reason; except, alas, that it comes before the age of discretion.

But Paine had one point of superiority to the mere Radicals then rising in England, who shared his cocksure rationalism and sublime superficiality. He was not merely commercial, any more than Shelley; and he seems to have had his doubts about the hopefulness of mere huckstering and unhampered exchange, somewhat in the manner of Cobbett. Now Cobbett, in his first American period, was hitting out at the Jacobins on the principle of 'see a head and hit it'; and the intellectual brow of Thomas Paine was naturally prominent. He attacked Paine as he generally did attack people, in a highly personal and ferocious manner.

He said things about that ingenuous Deist that were certainly quite false; Cobbett was not guilty of lying, but he was guilty of readily thinking evil. To him at that time Tom Paine was simply the Age of Reason; that is, the Age of Red Ruin. For Cobbett also was as simple as Tom Paine; and especially at that time he had as guileless a faith in Royalism as the other had in Republicanism. But when Cobbett came back to America after his imprisonment, he had made the terrible discovery that terminates youth, even if it often gives a new interest to life; the discovery that it is a strange world, that timings are not what they seem, and certainly not always what they profess to be. He was in a position to begin to admit that there might be more in Tom Paine than met the eye, especially the blind eye that he had turned on all the enemies of the English crown. But above all he went to America with his head still buzzing like a beehive with all sorts of new notions and suspicions, which went to make up the really original political philosophy of his later years. He was becoming a sceptic, not about crowns and creeds but about timings that the world round him reverenced far more than any creed or crown. He was doubting things that Whigs and Tories and Radicals were more and more taking for granted; the whole basis of the commercial success of his country. Just as he was questioning the very medium of their exchange, so he was questioning the very language of their controversy. He thought that paper money was waste paper; and he thought that industrial wealth was really only industrious waste. He doubted above all the abstract and invisible, we might say the transcendental, part of modern capitalism; the national debts and the international loans. Tom Paine took on a comparatively easy job when he attacked the Church. Will Cobbett had the inconceivable impudence to attack the Bank. Then he knew he was in collision with the colossal force of the whole modern world, like a man running with his head down at an express train. The whole world would leave such a lunatic to run alone; and Cobbett was left to run entirely alone. All the books and pamphlets of the period, and indeed all the books and pamphlets ever since, have scoffed at him about this part of his political adventure. He read such books and pamphlets with a face continually hardening into defiance and scorn; and then he made a strange discovery. In turning over, it may be, one out of twenty of the contemporary books and papers he was thus in the habit of tossing aside with a snort, not to say a snarl, he came upon some of the real writings of the atrocious Paine; and was astonished to find that some of the opinions of the atrocious Paine bore a remarkable resemblance to those of the just and public-spirited Cobbett. He found that Paine, of all men, and apparently alone among all men, had really tried to say some of these things that needed so excruciatingly to be said; and about which all mankind walked about gagged and in a ghastly silence. Surely it is not so very difficult to understand that he should have a revulsion as violent and impetuous as his original plunge of prejudice; surely those who have taken the trouble to write studies of Cobbett might have learned something of his manner of living, and how all his generosity and his vanity, his simplicity and his emotionalism, his sympathy for the under-dog and his fury at being himself the dupe, should have called clamorously in him for some vigorous external action for some proclamation or practical motion that should relieve the feelings and perhaps right the wrong. He had cruelly calumniated a man who might have been his friend and was certainly his ally. And it was too late to tell him so. For that which he had madly splashed with mud had already returned to dust, and Thomas Paine was dead.

Cobbett did something which any other age would have understood; nay, something that we should have understood if narrated of any other age. He was instantly possessed by a human impulse, which even the heathens have comprehended and only the humanitarians have denied. It brought him as it were at one stride to the grave of the man whose pardon he would have asked. The man had been buried in his land of exile; and Cobbett, himself an exile, realised as few could realise the horror of dying far away from home. He believed, as only he could believe, that the one perfect act of piety which could be done to the body of an Englishman was to bring it back to England. It seemed an absurd notion to men in the mercantile and rather materialistic mood of the beginning of the nineteenth century; it may well still seem absurd to many in the twentieth century. It would not seem absurd to men in the twelfth century. It will not seem absurd to men in the thirtieth or the fortieth century. It was felt to be incongruous with something comic and commonplace about contemporary manners; with the chimney-pot hats and the mutton-chop whiskers. But when men look back over long periods they have lost the contemporary derision of details and see only the main lines of humanity, and these acts of primitive ritual seem merely human. Aristophanes was a mighty mocker and derider of the details that were modern in his day; the wild hats and whiskers of ancient progress. Aristophanes was an enemy of modernity, and indeed of modernism. Aristophanes was also a lord of bad language, a man with all the splendid scurrility of Cobbett. But suppose it were recorded of Aristophanes that he came to repent of his satire on Euripides; suppose he had concluded too late that what he had taken for sophistry and scepticism had been a truer traditionalism. We should see nothing but beauty and pathos in some story about Aristophanes bringing the body of Euripides from some barbarian country to the temple of Athene. There would be nothing undignified or unworthy to be carved on a classic frieze in the figure of the great scoffer following the hearse of the great sceptic. But this is only because in the process of time the little things are lost and only the large lines remain. For that little flask of oil, with which the scoffer once stopped the mouth of the sceptic, has lost its bathos for us: and might well be the vessel of the sacred chrism for the anointing of the dead.

Cobbett was a son of the earth, or what used to be called a child of nature; and these rude anti-natural people are all ritualists. He had those giant gestures that are encouraged by the elbow-room of empty spaces and open skies; those impulses to send signals by instinctive posture and pantomime: to beckon, to brandish, to lift the head in battle or bow it at the graveside. He had in him also the mysticism of the mob; the mob that makes bonfires and burns men in effigy and chairs a man through the cheering streets on a chariot made of marching men. In all this impulsive imagery, and in another sense (I fear) than that in which it was said of Abraham Lincoln, he does truly and indeed belong to the ages. He belongs to all the ages except perhaps his own age. His own age certainly saw nothing but absurdity in his strange pilgrimage and his strange relics. The men with the chimney-pot hats could see nothing but the grotesque side of 'Cobby' lugging about as his luggage the bones of an old blasphemer in a box. And yet their idea of the grotesque in the matter is something of a paradox. For in a sense these people objected to ritual not because it was grotesque but because it was not grotesque. It was not grotesque enough to fit in with the grotesque hats and whiskers that were the fashion. The Utilitarians, like their fathers the Puritans, used ugliness as a uniform; that is, as a symbol. For the utilitarian ritual was not merely utilitarian. The chimney-pot hats were not really useful like chimney-pots. The mutton chop whiskers were not really sustaining like mutton chops. These also were a sort of black heraldry, like the black trappings of their funerals; but they symbolised the funeral of art or the old spontaneous symbolism. When a man used one of the gestures of that more generous symbolism they were offended with him and considered him ludicrous. But they were really offended with him for not being so ludicrous as themselves.

This itch or instinct for representative action, for ritual that goes beyond words like an embrace or a blow, was that part of Cobbett's character which was always reaching backwards to the medieval England that has never lost the name of Merry England. He was a man born out of due time, and forced to live and suffer in a world of mechanical traffic going to Manchester; when he ought to have ridden with Chaucer to Canterbury. His heraldry was sometimes deliberately grotesque, but it was always heraldic. When he hung up the gridiron outside his house in Kensington, he not only repeated the ritual of all the old shop signs and inn signs, but that of the crests and banners. But it was this in him that brought him into sympathy with another people whom he began to understand; and a remark of Peel aptly illustrates how little that understanding was understood.

Sir Robert Peel was a man who had stupidity in the soul. It went, as it often does, along with all the talents of a man of business and a man of the world.

He was the kind of man who only knows things by their labels, and has not only no comprehension but no curiosity touching their substance or what they are made of. A supreme example of this is to be found in this phase of the life of Cobbett. Peel seems to have suggested that nothing could seemingly be more impossible, nothing certainly more absurd, than a combination between Cobbett and O'Connell. And the reason he gave was that O'Connell was a Roman Catholic and Cobbett had brought back the bones of Tom Paine, who was an infidel. In other words, O'Connell was labelled a Papist and Paine was labelled a blasphemer and Cobbett was saddled with his bones as a sort of joke in the comic papers. This is the kind of folly that makes the fool walk like a mystical figure through the pages of the Book of Proverbs. If the man who said it had ever caught one glimpse of the inside of things, of the inside of men's minds, of the intrinsic implications of men's religions, he would have seen something that might have surprised him. The truth is that in all public life at that moment there was only one public man who could possibly understand and sympathise with the business of poor Paine's bones; and that man was Daniel O'Connell the Liberator. Any Catholic understands the idea of penitence taking the form of penance; if it be only natural penitence for a wrong done to a naturalistic philosopher. Any Catholic understands the idea of penance taking the form of public penance, and all the more if it really has in it something of humiliation. But above all O'Connell had the best reasons in the world for knowing that, in the English atmosphere of the moment, any attempt at such a public penance would really be accompanied by the simplest form of humiliation: that of being laughed at. He knew much better than most people that England in that mood thought such public penance theatrical. The business of the death of D'Esterre was in many ways a curious parallel to that of the burial of Paine. O'Connell in his youth had shot a man dead in a duel; and his perfectly sincere remorse led him to swear never again to accept a challenge, and to wear on his right hand a white glove to remind himself of his sin, especially when he took Sacrament. The refusal of challenges provided his political opponents with a conveniently safe man to challenge. And the wearing of the white glove was a piece of dramatic symbolism which naturally offended the plain sobriety and simple modesty of the young Disraeli. But O'Connell was well aware that, even among ordinary Englishmen, there was not one in a thousand who understood what his public gesture meant. It is possible that their fathers might have understood it. It is possible that their fathers did not think Henry the Second was merely striking a melodramatic attitude when he was scourged at the tomb of the saint he had martyred. But anyhow the sentiments of O'Connell were equally simple, too simple to be understood. Morbid as his scruple may seem to those who lament the murderous habits of the Irish, it really did seem to O'Connell a serious thing to have killed a man. Morbid as the other scruple may seem to those who are always reviling that demagogue for reviling everybody, it really did seem to Cobbett a serious thing to have libelled a man. That his sorrow for wrongdoing was highly intermittent and inconsistent is very true; but he scarcely stands alone among his fellow creatures in that respect. But not to see that there was a reason for remorse in the case of Paine is to be blind to the whole case of Cobbett. Cobbett was shouting in deafening tones to deaf ears a certain warning of danger; a danger he alone could see, or at least a danger in which no one else would believe. He believed that the whole financial network of national debts and paper money would eventually drag England to destruction. He may have been wrong; though in fact it is far easier now than it was then to maintain that he was right. But anyhow, believing this, he found that almost the only other Englishman who had warned England, or helped him to save England, was an Englishman whom he had himself slandered and might even have silenced by mistake. If there be any man who does not understand his feeling the need of a public apology to such a solitary and silent ally, such a man is very much less of a man than William Cobbett or Daniel O'Connell or Thomas Paine.

Anyhow, as things stood, he could get no more good out of the possible sympathy of O'Connell than out of the inevitable contempt of Peel. His political friendships, as we have noted, were very unstable and unsatisfactory; not so much, as is often supposed, because Cobbett changed his opinion, as because nobody else ever really understood the fundamental opinion that he did not change. The fellowship he did afterwards establish with O'Connell was more genuine than most; but that also was disturbed by quarrels. In one case, curiously enough, Cobbett was more O'Connellite than O'Connell. He fiercely (and perhaps rightly) blamed the Liberator for accepting a compromise suited to the more reactionary Irish bishops. His quarrel with Hunt dates originally from his second visit to America, from which he sent word, in his reckless way, repudiating some letter of which he had forgotten the details, and which contained a charge against the domestic morals of Hunt, whom Cobbett did not then even know. Yet even the misunderstanding is of the sort that wants understanding. Many of the Radicals really were cut off from Cobbett by a deep difference about morals; and anybody who thinks the Radical Programme must look a larger thing than the institution of marriage does not know what the story of Cobbett is all about.

One of his grim jokes called the English Grammar belongs to this second period of his American exile. Most people who have seen the title have probably avoided the book; under the lamentable delusion that the English Grammar is an English Grammar. Yet it is eminently characteristic of the author that it really is among other things an English Grammar. If it is a joke, it is not a practical joke in the sense of an April Fool joke; which may be defined as a hilarious disappointment. Cobbett really sets out to teach the structure of our language with all the dry earnestness of which only the self-educator is capable, and with all the direct lucidity of which he almost alone was capable. It is the very fact that he has got so completely into the swing of scholastic demonstration that gives a sort of absent-minded insolence to his offhand allusions and illustrations, which is something rather unique in literature. He will say, merely for the sake of illustration, of course, something like, 'You must never, for instance, fall into the vulgarity of using the word as it is used by the Archbishop of Canterbury in the following passage'; or, 'The following remarks by the Duke of Wellington illustrate this ignorant habit'; or, 'You will not fall into the ludicrous error of the Prime Minister, when he says,' and so on. It is as if a rather strict and precise schoolmaster were demonstrating on the blackboard and drawing geometrical figures for his class, in the presence of the school governors or inspectors or other distinguished visitors. It is as if he were to go on calmly drawing on the blackboard, but drawing caricatures of these eminent strangers without altering his attitude or the tone of his voice as he talked calmly over his shoulder. As we shall notice more generally later, this sort of thing was symbolic. Cobbett was thought to lack a sense of proportion; but there were many who wished he had less of a sense of humour. In some ways he was really simple; but in other ways he was less simple than he seemed. He was less simple than the simple person whom he hoped to see opening the English Grammar with the pure and stainless intention of learning his regular verbs. As he read on from the exposition of irregular verbs to that of very irregular verbalisms, there might gradually dawn on that simple pupil two curious and almost uncanny facts: first, that the teacher was white-hot with anger, and, second and stranger still, that he was not angry with his pupil. But the pupil might begin to understand that the teacher was rather more of an artist in anger than many suppose. Many might dismiss the English Grammar by saying that the English are too English to have any grammar, and that Cobbett was too English to invent one. But his logic was sometimes almost French in its lucidity; and in denouncing the bigwigs he did really prove them illogical, though he knew it would annoy them much more to prove them ungrammatical. A good example occurred just after Cobbett's second return to England at about this time. When he was to speak at Manchester the authorities had sent a solemn warning to him, forbidding him to make a public entry into the town, or holding him responsible for any riotous results of such an action. He turned on them and rent them with perfect reasonableness. Perhaps it would be too much, at any time, to describe his reasonableness as sweet reasonableness. 'What do you mean by a public entrance? If I come into your town at all I must come in in a carriage or on horseback or on foot'; for it was before the time of railways. He demanded to know whether they expected him to walk in with a tub over his head, in order to escape notice. I do not know whether any note was ever taken of the official answer; but the truth of the matter is that there is no answer. That is why the incident is a very good specimen of Cobbett's controversial style at its best; and why so many people would have liked to put his head in a tub, not to say a halter. For it is quite a mistake to suppose that his controversial method consisted merely of calling names. He did call names, and was rather addicted to inventing nicknames. Even then he was perhaps disliked less for inventing names than for ignoring titles. But so far from his argument always depending on words, he is constantly appealing from words to thoughts; and it is his opponents who are merely wordy. His style has a superficial air of being reckless, but it is not thoughtless. It is his official opponents who are thoughtless. It is the statesmen and the secretaries of state, the judges and the magistrates and the scholars, who are in the strict sense thoughtless. It is none the less strictly true to say that they speak without thinking, although they may take a long time to think or to speak. And in most cases, when their minds at last begin to move with a majestic reluctance, they do say things of which that warning to Cobbett is a conspicuous example. They talk journalese because they think journalese. That phrase about a public entrance is a model utterance of the man who does not know what he means. He had a vague image in his mind of something happening that he would not like; a lot of damned people cheering that damned demagogue. He objected to a public entry because it would be a popular entry; and it never occurred to him to think out the simple question of whether the damned demagogue could prevent it being public or prevent it being popular. These trifling incidents are only interesting as illustrating the point of this pointed mode of speech: the fact that in nine cases out of ten it was his enemies who used mere words, and he who appealed to the meaning of words; it was his enemies whose language was rhetorical in the sense of not being real. It was he who was thoughtful, though he thought too quickly; it was they who were thoughtless, though they thought too slow. This is the whole point, as in the case of the English Grammar. There is sometimes something almost cruel in the logical vigilance with which he pounces on the carelessness of the conventional. Conventional writers use heavy words so lightly; and he used light words so heavily: every homely word like a hatchet.

Another work of this period bore the fine title of *The Last Hundred Days of English Freedom*, attacking the coercion acts that had threatened his liberty in England. It is notable that Cobbett always treated tyranny as a new thing; his attitude to abstract revolution was well expressed in the phrase, 'I was born under a King and Constitution; but I was not born under the Six Acts.' It was a new Tory raid and reign of terror that had driven him into exile; but he did not remain there long; and his conduct when he returned showed he had no intention of being silent at home if he had been noisy abroad. An accident brought his change of plans to a head. His farm on Long Island was burned down; he moved first to New York, and finally from New York to England. He was given a public dinner and addressed a large meeting; perhaps it is ironical that his only immediate difficulty was bringing the bones of Paine through the custom-house. I wonder what he said when asked if he had anything to declare.

So for the second time William Cobbett came back across the Atlantic to the harbours of his own land. It would be easy to insist on a picturesque contrast between the two voyages. Doubtless, if somebody had told him on his first voyage that he would make the second voyage in the character of the chief mourner for Tom Paine, he might well have thrown that obliging prophet into the sea. On the first occasion he had returned to receive what truly might be called a royal welcome; a royal welcome from Royalists. He had come back to be toasted by the gentlemen of England, talking over their wine of his services to the Tory cause, of the blows that their loyal yeoman could deal at Boney and the Yanks. He had come back the second time, the demagogue of a darker hour, to meet a roar of angry admiration from the strikers and frame-breakers of the smoky north as well as the potential rick-burners of the agrarian war; the Titan of the English Revolution. At least if any man could have made an English revolution, if any hour in our history could really have been revolutionary, the hour was come and the man.

And yet he was exactly the same man. He was the same solid figure, with his sober good-humoured face and small shrewd eye; and in the depths of his mind, I fancy, no difference at all. It is difficult to talk of his inner consciousness, for nobody ever went there, least of all himself. But if it were penetrated, I fancy it would be found to be filled with a vast void of innocence that wondered and questioned, and was a little puzzled by the answers to its questions as is a child by the inconsistencies or quarrels of its parents. Enormous queries, as elementary as nursery riddles, would have been found to fill that void. What was wrong? and how could it be wrong to be right? Why must not a soldier object to soldiers being starved by swindlers? Why must not a patriot object to their being flogged by foreigners? Why ought not a Tory to dislike squires being driven out by stockbrokers? Why ought not a Radical to dislike peasants being oppressed by Jews? Why did a man find himself in the House of Lords if he cheated the nation, and in Newgate if he tried to point out that it was cheated? As he gazed at the great expanses of that empty and shining sea, it may be that there was an interlude in his incessant mental activity of mere recrimination and retort, that the clouds of too much controversy cleared a little, and he became half conscious of why he was so incurably himself. But even so there would only have been found, like some strange sunrise under the sea, under his all too salt humour and all the waters of bitterness that had gone over him, a lucid and enduring surprise.

V

THE AMATEUR HISTORIAN

There is a joke with which we are all familiar, about the rustic who relates some local legend, as of a hero who hurled a huge rock into a river, and who says that it must be true because the rock is still there. As is commonly the case in the small talk of a scientific age, the satire is directed against popular ideas. As is also commonly the case in such an age, the satire is really very shallow. When the critics mock a man for saying, 'I believe it because I have seen the rock,' nine-tenths of them could not give any sort of reason for their own historic beliefs, beyond saying, 'I believe it because I saw it somewhere set out in printer's ink by somebody I never knew, referring to evidence I have never seen, and telling a tale which I cannot test in any way whatever, even by the look of the landscape.' The rustic does not rely merely on the rock but on the tradition – that is, the truthfulness of a certain sort of people, many of whom he has known. But at least the rock and the river do fit in with the tradition; and to that limited extent consistency is corroboration. It is far more superstitious to assume that print is proof. So far as print is concerned, the whole of history might be as utterly imaginary as that mazy river and that dancing rock in the dizzy pipedream of 'Kubla Khan.'

But there are others whose state of mind is still more extraordinary. They not only do not need the landscape to corroborate their history, but they do not care if the landscape contradicts their history. They are not content with the very reasonable statement that the existence of the rock does not prove the existence of the hero. They are so anxious to show that there was no hero, that they will shut their eyes and say there is no rock. If the map marks the place as a waterless desert, they will declare it is as dry as a bone, though the whole valley resound with the rushing river. The whole huge rock will be invisible, if a little book on geology says it is impossible. This is at the opposite extreme to the irrational credulity of the rustic, but it is infinitely more irrational. It is not inferring something from the rock that the rock does not prove; it is denying what the rock does prove. Or rather it is denying what the rock is; that ultimate and terrible rock of reality, that veritable rock of offence, against which all delusions will dash themselves to pieces. This great delusion of the prior claim of printed matter, as something anterior to experience and capable of contradicting it, is the main weakness of modern urban society. The chief mark of the modern man has been that he has gone through a landscape with his eyes glued to a guidebook, and could actually deny in the one anything that he could not find in the other. One man, however, happened to look up from the book and see things for himself; he was a man of too impatient a temper, and later he showed too hasty a disposition to tear the book up, or toss the book away. But there had been granted to him a strange and high and heroic sort of faith. He could believe his eyes.

William Cobbett was pre-eminently a man with eyes in his head. He had of course other human attributes; such as a tongue in his head. Many considered it a merely bitter or blasphemously seditious tongue; but it was a tongue that could sometimes be for great mobs like the tocsin from a great tower. But when all emotional effects of such demagogy or deafening sensationalism have died away, the impression that will remain longest in the mind is the quiet and constant use that he made of his eyes. It is as if, after all passions had chased each other like shadows across his face, we saw his face at last in repose and realised that he had the eyes of a sailor; the eyes that can see a dot or speck on the distant horizon. But he could see dots and specks in the foreground as well. He could focus his sight at many different ranges; an organic power which is the point of what Carlyle said of somebody else, that he had eyes and not merely spectacles. Because his eyes were sharp they were clear; because his sight was exact it was even subtle. At its best it could really measure things, and even the degrees of things. It could place anything from the face of a stranger to the strength of a horse; from the shade of ripeness in a cornfield to the shade of rottenness in a Cabinet Minister. The ultimate impression of his personality is not so much of violence as of vigilance. So strong is this impression, that anyone who has been long in his literary company cannot shake off an uncanny impression of being watched. He cannot help fancying that this man who has been dead a hundred years has his eye on events in England and may suddenly speak – probably not in an amiable manner. It is as if, in some elfin tale, those strange eyes in one man's head were stars that could survive him.

But there is one particular form of this faculty in Cobbett which is not so sharply apprehended; and perhaps is not so easy to apprehend. For in this sense it is a faculty which few people, if any people, fully possess in the urban population of today. It is destroyed rather than helped by the urban education of today. Cobbett was very far from being an enemy of education. He was, as has been said elsewhere, a great educationist. He published French and English grammars of his own composition, and exhorted all young people to learn. Here and there he even showed a touch of that too crude and earnest respect for education which so often marks the self-educated man. But for all that, he had a native power or piece of good fortune which education never gives and sometimes destroys. In one thing he was a very lucky and lonely mortal.

He could see before he could read. Most modern people can read before they can see. They have read about a hundred things long before they have seen one of them. Most town children have read about corn or cattle as if they were dwarfs or dragons, long before they have seen a grain of wheat or a cow. Many of them have read about ships or churches, or the marching of soldiers or the crowd cheering a king, or any other normal sight, which they have never seen. By a weird mesmerism which it is not here necessary to analyse, what people read has a sort of magic power over their sight. It lays a spell on their eyes, so that they see what they expect to see. They do not see the most solid and striking things that contradict what they expect to see. They believe their schoolmasters too well to believe their eyes. They trust the map against the mountain. Cobbett was a man without these magic spectacles. He did not see what he expected to see, but what he saw. He liked books; but he could not only read between the lines but through the book.

Now, in nothing is this more vivid than in his vision of history. Most of us know what was the accepted general version of English history when we were at school; at any rate when I was at school, and still more, of course, when Cobbett was at school – in so far as he was ever at school. England had emerged out of a savage past to be the greatest empire in the world, with the best-balanced constitution in the world, by a wise and well-timed progress or series of reforms, that ever kept in mind the need of constitutionalism and of balance. The Barons had extorted a constitutional charter from the King, in advance of that feudal age and a foundation for parliamentary freedom. The Commons came into the struggle for parliamentary freedom when it was waged against the Stuarts. By that time the Revival of Learning had led to the Reformation or sweeping away of the superstition that had been the only religion of the ruder feudal time. This enlightenment favoured the growth of democracy; and though the aristocrats still remained, and remain still, to give dignity to the state with their ancient blazonry of the Conquest and the Crusades, the law of the land is no longer controlled by the lords but by the citizens. Hence the country has been filled with a fresh and free population, made happy by humane and rational ideas, where there were once only a few serfs stunted by the most senseless superstitions. I ask anyone if that is not a fair summary of the historical education in which most modern people over forty were brought up. And having read it first, we went to look at the towns and castles and abbeys afterwards, and saw it or tried to see it. Cobbett, not having read it, or not caring whether he had read it, saw something totally different. He saw what is really there.

What would a man really see with his eyes if he simply walked across England? What would he actually see in the solid farms and towns of three-quarters of the country, if he could see them without any prejudice of historical interpretation? To begin with, he would see one thing which Cobbett saw, and nobody else seems ever to have seen, though it stared and still stares at everybody in big bulk and broad daylight. He would find England dotted with a vast number of little hamlets consisting entirely of little houses. Considered as little houses there is much that might be said about them both critical and sympathetic. They are generally picturesque cottages; they are often what is described as picturesque tumble-down cottages. They are the most beautiful houses in the world for all appreciative people who have ever been outside them. For the less obvious and outstanding people who have always been inside them, it would be an exaggeration to say that they are the most beautiful houses in the world. About these people inside also a great deal that is good and bad might be said; they are kindly and full of English humours and all the virtues that belong to an atmosphere of ale. But they are not citizens and do not want to be; they have hardly even heard of the word. They can no more imagine the vanishing of the squire than the vanishing of the sky; though they may grumble at the moods of both. But anyhow the point is that their houses are little houses, and especially low houses; so that a tall man walking past them would sometimes have to stoop down under the eaves to peer into the front window, as if he were travelling in a town of the dwarfs. And the town is a very little town; often only a handful of houses to be counted on the fingers.

In the midst of this little cluster or huddle of low houses rises something of which the spire or tower may be seen for miles. Relatively to the roofs beneath it, the tower is as much an exception as the Eiffel Tower. Relatively to the world in which it was built, it was really an experiment in engineering more extraordinary than the Eiffel Tower. For the first Gothic arch was really a thing more original than the first flying-ship. And indeed something of its leap and its uplifting seems to make architecture akin to aviation. Its distant vaulted roof looks like a maze of mathematical patterns as mysterious as the stars; and its balance of fighting gravitations and flying buttresses was a fine calculation in medieval mathematics. But it is not bare and metallic like the Eiffel Tower or the Zeppelin. Its stones are hurled at heaven in an arc as by the kick of a catapult; but that simple curve has not the mere cruelty of an engine of war. The whole building is also a forest of images and symbols and stories. There are saints bringing their tales from all the towns and countries in Europe. There are saints bearing the tools of all the trades and crafts in England. There are traces of trade brotherhoods as egalitarian as trades unions. There are traditions of universities more popular than popular education. There are a thousand things in the way of fancy and parody and pantomime; but with the wildest creative variety it is not chaotic. From the highest symbol of God tortured in stone and in silence, to the last wild gargoyle flung out into the sky as a devil cast forth with a gesture, the whole plan of that uplifted labyrinth shows the mastery of an ordered mind.

It is the parish church, and it is often very old; for it was built in the days of darkness and savage superstition. The picturesque cottages are all of much later date; for they belong to the ages of progress and enlightenment.

If people saw the Great Pyramid and found scattered about its base a few patchwork tents of a few ragged Bedouins, they would hardly say there had been no civilisation in that land until the Bedouins brought it. Yet a Pyramid is as plain as a post of wood compared with the dizzy balance and delicate energy of the Gothic. If they had seen some dingy tribe of barbarians living in their little mud huts, when high above their heads went the soaring arch of a Roman aqueduct almost as remote as the rainbow, they would hardly say that the Romans must have been savages and that the savages alone were civilised. Yet the round Roman arch is really rudimentary compared with the prism of forces in the pointed Gothic arch. But the truth is that the Catholics, having some humility even in their hatred, never did make this absurd pretence that paganism was barbaric, as their enemies afterwards made the absurd pretence that Catholicism was barbaric. They denounced the wickedness of the world, but they recognised the Pyramids and the Coliseum as wonders of the world. It was only the great medieval civilisation whose conquerors were base enough to pretend that it had not been a civilisation at all. But that is not the aspect of the case immediately important here. The point immediately important here is that this solid stone object did and does stand up among the others like a mountain among molehills: and that nobody could see it but Cobbett. We talk of not seeing the wood for the trees; but one would think anybody could see a poplar tree in spite of the presence of six rhododendron trees. Yet we may repeat, in a spiritual but most realistic sense, that nobody except Cobbett could see the church spire.

He did not by any means see all that was to be seen in the church, or all that has here been noted in the church. For that he would really have required more education; and not the sort of education that he could then have got merely by being educated. He was a simple man in a rationalistic age, and he saw something. It was something very primitive and elementary; but he saw it. He saw the size. He tells us again and again that he has found a village of which the whole present population could be put into the porch of the village church, leaving the whole vast and varied interior as empty and useless as Stonehenge. What had become of all the people? Why should anybody, in any age, pay to build a church serving two thousand people when he only had to serve twenty people? Was it true, could it be true, after all, that the population of England had so hugely increased from what had once been a mere handful? Was it only that the new towns had hugely increased, leaving the countryside a mere wilderness? And could it be true that the men who built such things were a sort of Pictish dwarfs or troglodytes of the twilight, when what they had left looked so like the houses of a generation of giants, which could not even be filled with a generation of dwarfs?

These doubts had much to do with historical and social views of Cobbett to be considered in their order; but in the first place they are to be noted as a working model of his power to see things simply and as they stand. Hundreds of elegant essayists and artists had traced the more graceful proportions of Gothic buildings, vaguely regarding them as ruins. The end of the eighteenth century is full of these painters in watercolours and first cousins to the Earl of Cork. What Cobbett saw was not the graceful proportions but rather the disgraceful disproportions. He saw a colossal contrast; the contrast between a village that was hardly a hamlet and a village church that was almost a cathedral. It was the biggest and baldest of all the facts; and yet it was the fact that nobody else saw. The others did not see it because they had been educated not to see it; because they had been educated to see the opposite. Since liberty and light had come to the Commons with the Whig revolution, the Commons must somewhere or other be free and enlightened; they could not still be living in hovels under the shadow of a huge old church. There had been nothing before that revolution but feudal ferocity and priest craft. So, somehow or other, somebody had built the church by sheer ferocity; or priest craft can be made a complete substitute for every other craft, including the craft of the sculptor and the stonemason. But Cobbett began with the big fact that he could see with his own eyes, and with that he contrived, with tremendous reconstructive power, to turn all English history upside down.

His view involved another truth that may be symbolised by another building. When we said that there was nothing but small houses to compete with the church, we meant of course that there was nothing else within the immediate circuit of the church: that the village church was the only big building in the village. There was another very big building at some distance from the village which bulked very much larger in the minds of the villagers. Indeed, it might be said that they lived in the material shadow of the church and in the moral shadow of the country house. Now the example of the squire's house is yet another which illustrates the illusion that is general and the realism that is exceedingly rare. All that Cobbett could have read in books, all that he could have learnt at school, would have taught him a view of the manor-house or country seat which is still a commonplace in novels and newspapers. It is almost literally a view; in the sense of a landscape seen in the mind's eye. But men only see that sort of view by shutting their eyes. Cobbett formed his views by opening his eyes. The universal impression or illusion was that the Tory squires were an ancient aristocracy, full of feudal notions and Norman blood; and from this it followed logically that they lived in castles or at any rate in moated granges, Tudor manor-houses, and other ancient and appropriate haunts. If Cobbett had believed in historical novels, or in the histories that were all on the same model as the historical novels, he would have gone about looking for the Castle of Otranto in the valleys of England: and never seen the little temple that Horace Walpole really stuck up for himself on the top of Strawberry Hill.

But Cobbett had this strange power of faith: he could believe his eyes. Most people cannot believe their eyes; it is the very last thing in which they can believe. They can believe in the wildest creeds and the crudest philosophies; similarly they can believe in a past made up of *The Castle of Otranto* and *The Mysteries of Udolpho*. But they cannot believe in the present; in the thing present to their sight; in the thing in whose real presence they stand. But Cobbett really had this unearthly detachment, this dry light of reality, this vision of a man from the moon. In that light he probably saw what the country houses are really like; as he certainly saw what the parish churches are really like. Here and there there is really a castle; now generally a showplace. Here and there there is really an old Tudor manor, often preserved as carefully as a model in a museum. But the house of the squire dominating a hundred countrysides all over England is something quite different; something quite unmistakable; and something to a large extent uniform. It is emphatically a rule, where the romantic castles and manors are exceptions. It is a rule in more senses than one; for the populace has the squire for a landlord, for an employer, and, it may be added, for a judge; for the magistracy is made up of the gentry. Anyhow, the house has a positive character which amounts to a pattern.

It really looks rather like a large public building from a large city exiled in the provinces. It looks like a Town Hall taken away on the wings of the fairies, and set down far away in the woodlands. It looks like a Palais de Justice rusticating for some reason or other and taking a ramble in the country. It is not only very large, but it does not *look* like a private house at all. It is like something conscious that it is a seat of government and power over men – as it is. It is nothing like so cosy as a castle. It is rather open in the same sense as a law court. Above all, it is built in the same style as the average modern law court. What makes that style important is its *date*. Very few of the real country seats are really of a Tudor type; hardly any are of a medieval type. The type and pattern of them is of a sort that bears the stamp of a subsequent and clearly marked epoch of society. Generally they are Georgian houses; often they are rather earlier, and correspond to the quainter style of William of Orange and Queen Anne. But nearly all belong to what the French call the Classic Age; meaning that stretch of the seventeenth and eighteenth centuries in which the full result of the Renaissance worked itself out, becoming if anything more and more classical until its shell was broken by the Romantic movement and the French Revolution. In short, the whole architecture is the recent creation of a rationalistic age. It belongs as much to the Age of Reason as the books of Voltaire.

But people were blinded to this fact by books they knew better than those of Voltaire. Every novel and novelette told them that a bad baronet lived in a castellated tower; and they could not see that he lived in a sort of comfortable classic temple. Tennyson, calling in his youth on the Lady Clara Vere de Vere, suffered the delusion of seeing a lion on her old stone gates. Most probably it was really a nymph or an urn. For that matter, Tennyson would probably have made some curious discoveries if he had looked more closely into Lady Clara's claims to Norman blood, however it might be with her claims to coronets. But for the moment I am speaking simply of things seen, or rather of things not seen. I am speaking of the veil which our version of history hangs between us and the real facts about our fathers, even the facts in front of our eyes. Very few people saw that the aristocratic country house is commonly a comparatively new building, and looks more like a General Post Office than a feudal fortress. Such ornament as it has is a curious cold exuberance of heathen nymphs and hollow temples. Because it stands for the age of the sceptics, its gods are not only dead but have never been alive. Its gardens are full of shrines without idols or idols without idolaters.

Finally, as has been hinted already, there does exist a third historic memorial and variety of architecture or the use of architecture. Among these aristocratic houses and estates, setting aside such curiosities as castles, there does appear fairly commonly one type of country house that really is old and really is medieval. The medieval part of it is often in ruins, and only valued because it is in ruins. But the ruins have the same soaring and skyward lines as those of the large and empty parish church. Yet the house as a whole is by no means a ruin, but is turned into a country house quite as comfortable, or rather luxurious, as the more common pattern of the Georgian houses. But the very name of that house of luxury remains a medieval name; and a very queer name too.

We should think it rather odd if a profiteer had a country house that was called The Cathedral. We might think it strange if a stockbroker had built a villa and habitually referred to it as a church. But we can hardly see the preposterous profanity by which one chance rich man after another has been able to commandeer or purchase a house which he still calls an Abbey. It is precisely as if he had gone to live in the parish church; had breakfasted on the altar, or cleaned his teeth in the font. That is the short and sharp summary of what has happened in English history; but few can get it thus foreshortened or in any such sharp outline. Anyhow, this third type of monument of the past does offer itself visibly to the eye like the other two. The romantic reactionary at the end of the eighteenth century might not often find the Bad Baronet in a castle, but might really find him in an abbey. The most attractive of all such reactionaries, Miss Catherine Morland, was not altogether disappointed in her search for the Mysteries of Udolpho. She knew at least that General Tilney lived in an abbey; though even she could hardly have mistaken General Tilney for an abbot. Nor was she wrong in supposing that a crime had been committed by that gentleman in Northanger Abbey. His crime was not being an abbot. But Jane Austen, who had so piercing a penetration of the shams of her own age, had had a little too much genteel education to penetrate the shams of history. Despite the perverse humour of her juvenile *History of England*, despite her spirited sympathy with Mary Stuart, she could not be expected to see the truth about the Tudor transition. In these matters she had begun with books, and could not be expected to read what is written in mere buildings and big monuments. She was educated, and had not the luck to be self-educated like Cobbett. The comparison is not so incongruous as it may seem. They were the four sharpest eyes that God had given to the England of that time; but two of them were turned inward into the home, and two were looking out of the window. I wish I could think that they ever met.

Anyhow, all this is written in large letters of stone and clay across the land; in a giant alphabet of arch and column and flying buttress. And these three striking things stand out to tell the main tale of English history, even to a man who had never opened a book. The first is a very ancient and artistically beautiful parish church, far too big for its parish. The second is an aristocratic mansion of much later date, and looking like the palace of a German prince of the eighteenth century. The third is a similar palace constructed out of the ruins, if not of a similar parish church, at least of a religious building similar to the parish church. With those three solid facts alone a man might have pieced together the truth that no historians would tell him. Somehow or other there had once been a larger religious life which was also a popular life. Somehow or other its memorials had been taken over by a new race of men, who had become great lords in the land, and had been able to disdain alike the people and the religion.

Cobbett was an amateur historian in that sense; that he used his own wits. Those who sniff at such amateur history are not using theirs. They say the amateur's views cannot be correct, because they are not founded on research. In other words, they say he cannot see what is there, because he sees what is obviously there. He cannot have seen the sun, because he evidently did not have to extract the sunbeams from cucumbers. He cannot have really understood that two and two make four, because he understood it at once. But allowing for this, such academic characters underrate even the detailed information of men like Cobbett. It must once more be emphasised very strongly that Cobbett did not in the least despise books. He had far too much common sense to despise any common and convenient way of obtaining information. He was the very reverse of the sort of sentimental reactionary who thinks that all humanity would be innocent if only it were illiterate. But he did not allow what he read to contradict what he had seen. And when he really began to read, he found that what he read confirmed what he had seen.

I say he really began to read; for there is a distinction in this case. It is not merely a question of the books, but rather of the books behind the books. The fashionable book of history is at best little better than a leading article; it is founded on the documents as a leading article is founded on the news; in both cases a rather careful selection. Like a leading article the historical summary is generally partisan; and never quite so partisan as when it professes to be impartial. Cobbett had to go a little deeper than these superficial summaries to trace in the past the truths he had already discovered in the present. It was a fortunate coincidence that it was precisely at this time that the most learned and laborious of English historians produced the work on which so many other works have been founded. John Lingard was a very moderate man, but even the prejudices he was presumed to have gave him a detached position from the fashionable fallacies of that particular age. With a mass of material he established his own very moderate version of what had really happened in England; and by the use of that material Cobbett produced his own version, which some have hesitated to call moderate.

This was the celebrated *History of the Reformation*, published in 1824. The real question at issue about the *History of the Reformation* is not so much concerned with a certain state of things as with the right reaction to that state of things. What ought a man to do when he believes that public opinion has grown accustomed to repose confidently in a completely wrong picture of the past? A man might agree with Cobbett about the existence of the error, without in the least agreeing with Cobbett about the proper process of the enlightenment.

The very name of Lingard is enough to prove the possibility. Lingard had a strong case, and deliberately understated the case to give a greater impression of impartiality. Cobbett had the same strong case, and deliberately flung away all such airs of impartiality to prove how completely he had been convinced. When Cobbett found that what he conceived to be a truth had been concealed by a trick, his reaction was a towering passion; and whether that or a more patient exposition be appropriate to controversy, there is no doubt about which is appropriate to Cobbett. He would have said that when he found a man robbing his hen-roost he called out 'Stop, thief!' and not 'Stop, philosophical communist invading the thesis of private property!' He would have said that when a man told lies he called him a liar, and not a person insensible to the value of objective reality. Yet it is probably true that many listened to Lingard who could not listen to Cobbett. And it is true to say that such persons could not hear him because he talked so loud. But as to questioning what he said – that is quite different and much more difficult. Those who suppose that he must be talking nonsense because he was talking too loud are much less clearheaded and even cool-headed than he was. Veracity has nothing to do with violence, one way or the other. One historian may prefer to say, 'The Emperor Nero set on foot several conspiracies against the life of Agrippina his mother, and expressed satisfaction when the final attempt was successful.' Another may say, 'The bloody and treacherous tyrant foully murdered his own mother, and fiendishly exulted in the detestable deed.' But the second statement records the same fact as the first, and records it equally correctly. It is accurate to say, 'The Rev. Titus Oates declared on oath his knowledge of a Papist conspiracy; but his statements, which led to the execution of many Papists, were subsequently found to be fictitious.' But it is every bit as accurate to say, 'The liar and perjurer Oates cruelly swore away the lives of innocent Catholics, blasphemously calling on God to witness to his murderous lie.' The violent man is telling the truth quite as logically and precisely as the more dignified man. It is a question of what we consider a superiority of literary form; not of any sort of superiority in historical fact. And this was substantially the chief difference between Cobbett and Lingard; not to mention all the modern scholars who are pupils of Lingard.

Cobbett stated all his facts in one prolonged and almost monotonous fury. But if he was wrong, he was wrong in his fury, not especially in his facts. There are many mistakes in his *History of the Reformation,* as there are in most histories; though most people did not even know what they were until they were carefully discovered and tabulated by Cardinal Gasquet. I doubt if there are so many of them as could be found by so good a scholar in all the more cautious and constitutional historians. Cobbett did not begin with whole masses of obvious myth and romance, like those which Macaulay criticised in Hume. He did not depend on the expurgated extravagances of manifestly mad sectarians, like those which Aytoun criticised in Macaulay. The truth is that the general impression that Cobbett wrote a wild romance is really only a general impression. It does not rest, and it never did rest, on the discovery of the particular points in which he was wrong. The impression was one of *paradox;* the mere fact that he seemed to be calling black white, when he declared that what was white had been blackened, or that what seemed to be white had only been whitewashed. But the shock came from the moral comment or application rather than from the definite details. For the definite details even then, very often, were not in dispute. For instance, it is supremely characteristic of Cobbett that he reversed the common titles by talking of Bloody Bess and Good Queen Mary. He could always find a popular phrase for an unpopular opinion. For he was always speaking to the mob, even when he was defying it. But this is an excellent example; for it is not shaken by any particular controversy about facts. Everybody knew even then that Queen Elizabeth was bloody, if pursuing people with execution and persecution and torture makes a person bloody; and that was the only reason for saying it of Mary. Everybody knew even then that Mary was good, if certain real virtues and responsibilities make a person good; a great deal more indubitably good than Elizabeth. It was the too obvious and biased *motive* of the inversion that irritated people. It was not really Cobbett's history that was in controversy; it was his controversialism. It was not his facts that were challenged; it was his challenge.

Here we are only concerned with his controversy as a part of his character. And of this sort of challenge we may almost say that it was the whole of his character. We must see the situation very simply, if we would see it as he saw it. He was simply a man who had discovered a crime: ancient like many crimes; concealed like all crimes. He was as one who had found in a dark wood the bones of his mother, and suddenly knew she had been murdered. He knew now that England had been secretly slain. Some, he would say, might think it a matter of mild regret to be expressed in murmurs. But when he found a corpse he gave a shout; and if fools laughed at anyone shouting, he would shout the more, till the world should be shaken with that terrible cry in the night.

It is that ringing and arresting cry of 'Murder!' wrung from him as he stumbled over those bones of the dead England, that distinguishes him from all his contemporaries. It is not the mere discovery of the bones, or in a sense even the study of them. It was not really, I repeat, the facts that were in dispute. The Gothic tower overhanging the modern cottage was as plain as a skeleton hanging on a gibbet. Some held that the bones were justly gibbeted; that the old England was fortunately dead. Others held that the bones were so old and decayed that they could now be the object of merely archaeological interest, like Egyptian mummies. What was peculiar to Cobbett was the way in which he treated this question of the past as a question of the present. He treated it, not as a historical point to be decided, but rather as a legal wrong to be righted. If he did not exactly answer the question, 'Can these dry bones live?' he did say in another sense, 'I know that their avenger liveth.' He was prepared to make those bones his business, like those of Paine; to be a detective in a mystery story, and present himself *ex ossibus ultor*. One might suppose a detective story would be more popular than an antiquarian essay;

and a charge of crime more lucid than a meditation on archaeology. Yet this was not wholly so; and the paradox is relevant to the whole riddle of Cobbett. The cry that rang through the startled village was loud but hardly clear. It may be that it was too loud to be clear.

It is possible to speak much too plainly to be understood. Most men with any convictions in a confused and complicated age have had the almost uncanny sensation of shouting at people that a mad dog is loose or the house is on fire, to be met merely with puzzled and painfully respectful expressions, as if the remark were a learned citation in Greek or Hebrew. For men in such an age are used to long words and cannot understand short ones. This comic sort of cross-purposes was especially the case with Cobbett. The world, in the sense of the ordinary political and literary world, could not understand him or what he said. People could not understand it because it was not obscure enough. It did not soothe them with those formless but familiar obscurities which they expected as the proper prelude to any political suggestion. He came to the point too quickly; and it deafened them like an explosion and blinded them like a flash of lightning. his rapidity produced all the effect of remoteness. People of this political and literary sort understood much better the speakers they were used to; or liked much better the speakers they did not understand. The pompous and polysyllabic felicities of the diction of Pitt seemed to them comforting if not comprehensible. The rich and loaded style of Burke seemed like some display of imperial wealth which could be admired though not calculated. It was the same with the literary as with the political utterance of the time. It was much easier to persuade people to listen to the merely romantic praise of the past as uttered by Scott than to the realistic praise of the past as uttered by Cobbett. Men vaguely felt that any sympathy with things thus lost in the mists of antiquity ought to be conveyed in more or less misty language, and with the air of one dealing with things not only dead but even unreal. It was more soothing to be told by a Great Enchanter what ghosts might haunt a ruined abbey than to be asked by a hard-headed bully of a yeoman how many people would fit into the porch of a parish church. Men found Melrose Abbey more visible by moonlight than their own parish church by daylight. The world will never pay its debt to the great genius of Walter Scott, who effected in European literature that second Renaissance that was called Romance. He opened those high dikes of mud that cut men off from the rivers of popular romantic tradition, and irrigated the dry garden of the Age of Reason. It is no disrespect to him to say that he was, like his own hero, an antiquary and at the same time a sceptic. But he was fashionable because he assured men that medievalism was only a romance; and Cobbett was far less fashionable when he urged it as a reality. Scott was merely sentimental about Mary Stuart, as he was about Charles Edward Stuart; he was singing 'Will ye no' come back again?' to people who would have been a horrible nuisance to him if they had come back again. But Cobbett was not sentimental about Mary Tudor; he did solidly believe that with her the good times went; and he did really want them to return.

Anyhow, when he revised history the revision really was a revelation. The revision may be revised, but it will not be reversed. The revelation may reveal itself further, but it will never hide itself again. Cobbett let the cat out of the bag; and this is none the less true because it was rather a wild cat when it came out of his bag. Nobody could pretend that because it was a wild cat it was a fabulous animal, when it was so obviously careering down the street. In other words, he drew attention to a fact; a fact which others have followed up and matched and balanced with other facts, a fact which others have restated more mildly or analysed more delicately, but still the original fact which he furiously asserted and his foes furiously denied. In so far as modern histories do really differ from the *History of the Reformation*, it is mostly because we have come to repeat with decorum what even he only dared to hurl with defiance. Ruskin and William Morris and many more pursued his path through that living labyrinth that had once been regarded as the dead shell of a village church. Maitland and Gasquet and many others justified by laborious study and annotation his wild but shrewd guesses about the greatness of medieval sociology. It was easy for them to state the medieval argument more mildly; simply because the modern audience had become more mild. But Cobbett's discovery can never be undiscovered; that is, it can never be covered up again. And that for the reason stated at the starting-point of this chapter.

A city that is set on a hill cannot be hid; a church set high above a city is even more hard to hide, when once it has been discovered. You cannot undiscover the elephant. That is why it is essential in this chapter to insist on the size and simplicity of the neglected thing, and the plain picture of the Surrey farmer standing staring at the village spire. Since Cobbett's historical conceptions have increasingly prevailed, there have been many attempts among the opponents of medieval ideals to get rid of this medieval renascence. There have been many efforts to explain away the elephant or minimise the cathedral. And they all fail by beginning at the trivial end and trying to chop inches off the elephant's tail; or seeking to set the ugliness of a gargoyle against the beauty of a cathedral. Thus they will pick this or that hole in the application of the Guild principle, without noticing that everything is conceded with the Guild principle itself; the simple fact that the principle of medieval trade was admittedly comradeship and justice, while the principle of modern trade was avowedly competition and greed. They will say that the Guild spirit was deficient in this and that; without beginning to touch the truth that we are deficient in the Guild spirit. In short, the attempts to rebut the revelations of medieval culture and creative reform are above all things trivial. They not only pick very small holes in a very large thing, but they do not seem to realise that the rest of the world can now look at the large thing as well as the small hole. But it was really William Cobbett, alighted from his horse, and standing for some idle moment in a church porch out of the rain, who first had a vision of this towering resurrection of a forgotten Christendom; and lifted up his eyes to things so lofty and remote that men had let them float unheeded over their heads like the tree-tops or the clouds. Perhaps the real story of Jack the Giant Killer is that Jack was the first man who was even tall enough to see the giant.

VI

THE RURAL RIDER

Even the most elementary sketches of Cobbett have tended to give too much of his biography and too little of his life. He had a picturesque career, if the pictures sometimes seemed to his critics to be comic pictures; he was always fighting, he was flung into gaol, he went wandering in foreign lands. And yet there was a sense in which everything he did was directed towards peace; a peace that he never fully gained. I have said that he swept across the country like a whirlwind; but in the heart of the whirlwind there is a calm. The picture in his own mind was a quiet picture; only, he was never left alone to enjoy it quietly. Perhaps it would be truer to say that he never left himself alone to enjoy it quietly. Anyhow, it was only occasionally in his wanderings through the world that he encountered the romantic adventure of staying at home. In the midst of his mind there was a secret landscape of field and farm under the evening light, which was continually being jerked out of the field of vision like a picture in a jolting camera. It is very difficult in practice to present the whole of his mind except as a fragmentary mind; but perhaps the most continuous scroll of all that he liked and thought about can be found in the long, rolling panorama of the *Rural Rides.*

A little while before the affair of his imprisonment he had taken a farm at Botley in Hampshire; where he lived for a time the sort of life he liked, spoiling his children and sparring with his neighbours; especially with the Botley parson. This reverend gentleman figured so prominently in Cobbett's satire as to become a sort of proverb; and yet the origin of a proverb is often difficult to trace. And it is by no means clear in what respect the infamy of the incumbent of Botley differed from that of other country clergymen. But he stands as a symbol of Cobbett's quarrel with the clergy of the Church of

England which in most of the other cases had other and more serious grounds. Two things may be noted, even at this stage, about his own rather curious sort of anti-clericalism. One is that if he scoffed at the Anglican clergy, he had not less but much more scorn and fury for the Dissenting Ministers and the Methodists and the Quakers. And second, that his first serious reason for dislike concerned the corruption of pluralism, and especially family favouritism. He execrated for economic reasons the large clerical families that kept their hold on a vast variety of livings and tithes. He was as yet unconscious that this road was leading him, past the comfortable vicarage which he cursed as he passed it, towards the gateway of a grey ruin that was still called an abbey.

In the confusion accompanying his great catastrophe, he had been obliged to sell his place at Botley; but much of his early life had radiated from there, and it makes a sort of starting-point for considering him in his capacity of a Rural Rider.

The *Rural Rides* are a landscape; but they are also a portrait. Sometimes we seem to be watching under rolling clouds the rolling country of the shires, valleys coloured like maps, or downs that seem to shoulder away the sky; and then again we are only looking at the changes on one stubborn face as it relapses into good humour or hardens into hate. That combination of the object and the subject is what makes writing into literature; and the *Rural Rides* are pure literature. Perhaps they are all the more literature because they might be counted loose and colloquial even for language. It would be a breathless experience even to hear a man talk in as slap-dash a style as Cobbett wrote; but the thing would be brilliant as well as breathless. Everything comes into this great soliloquy: details, dogmas, personalities, political debates, private memories, mere exclamations such as a man utters in really riding along a road. But through all there is the assumption that heaven has appointed him, or he has appointed himself (and perhaps he was too prone to confuse the conditions), to be a sort of national surveyor of the whole land of England and publish his report to the world. His notes simply as notes never fail to be amusing. Anybody with his wits about him may well read Cobbett for amusement, even when there is no question of agreement. He could make great buildings and even landscapes look ludicrous, like landscapes of topsy-turvydom, when he turned on them that Gargantuan grin. We shall note later how for him great London was simply 'the Wen,' a big boil and repulsive eruption on the body politic. We shall see how Old Sarum was 'the Accursed Hill.' He made the Martello towers look even sillier than they look now. Nothing was ever better in its way than the dramatic derision with which he pointed at the canal at Hythe, and told the people that this was meant to keep out the French armies that had just crossed the Rhine and the Danube. More questionable, but equally laughable, was his irreverent picture of the fortifications on the cliffs of Dover; which he described, with a sort of impudent innocence, as a hill full of holes to hide Englishmen from Frenchmen. So simple a view of the science of fortification it is perhaps needless to maintain; but even here we have the sort of cranky common sense that was never far distant from Cobbett, even when he was talking about what he did not in the least understand; as when he pointed out that it was very unlikely that the French would try to hand on a precipice at Dover when they had the whole flat stretch away to East Sussex and the levels of Rye and Pevensey, where all the conquerors had landed since history began.

He had hatreds that seemed too big for their object; like his loathing of tea and potatoes. But in his hate there was humour, and even conscious humour. Many social reformers who have a hankering after his principles would be much distressed by his prejudices. But it was one of his principles to have such prejudices. Nor indeed is it an unintelligent or unintelligible principle. He believed in the traditions of the past and the instincts of the people. And these things have always moved along generalisations, touching certain social types or local atmospheres. You cannot have that sort of common sense of the countryside if it is not allowed to say that Yorkshiremen are this or Kentish-men are that, or that one course is the best way with Gypsies or another the usual habit of Jews. Most people are still allowed to express these general impressions, until they come to the case of the Jews. There (for some reason I have never understood), the whole natural tendency has been to stop; and anybody who says anything whatever about Jews as Jews is supposed to wish to burn them at the stake. Cobbett was so exceedingly and almost alarmingly hearty in the expression of his dislikes that he can hardly be said to have laboured to remove the last impression. For anybody whose horror of persecution has not yet entirely destroyed his sense of humour, nothing could be more exhilarating than the passage in which Cobbett, having heard a Methodist preaching in a village, and being afterwards shown an antiquated pair of stocks on the village green, comments indignantly on the incongruity, the inconsequence, the intellectual outrage of having these two things so near to each other and not bringing the two things together into one harmonious whole.

The primary picturesqueness of his work has therefore something of the knockabout farce or even pantomime; like Mr Punch, he fights with the cudgel, the heavy but humorous and relatively even humane English weapon. When he hits our noble lords and learned judges such thundering cracks, we have the same causes of consolation as in the case of Punch and Judy. We have reason to know the weapon is made of wood. We have still better reason to know the heads are made of wood. All this superficial and broad farce must be allowed for first as part of the fun. He got a great deal of fun out of it, and we get a great deal of fun out of him; even if it is not only his foes who are made to look a little funny. But to be content with considering this pantomimic energy is to miss the paradox and therefore miss the point. The interesting thing is that this swashbuckler who, as we say, put on so much side had very notably another side; which might be called a soft side. But it was also decidedly a sober side. For instance, he who was the most impatient of men was the most patient of fathers. He was even the most patient of schoolmasters. The ploughman was capable of plodding as well as kicking. He could be not only soft but even subtle; and if we read the *Rural Rides* a second time, so to speak, we shall see certain things that are the moral of the book: and were never put there by a mere bully.

For instance, there is the educational element in him. Cobbett was a demagogue in the literal sense; that is, he was a demagogue in the dignified sense. He was a mob-leader; but he was not merely a man mob-led. He certainly was not a man merely seeking to ingratiate himself with the crowd, or indeed with anybody else. At least, if he were supposed to be ingratiating himself, he must be credited with a curious and original selection of words with which to do it. But the truth is that it was not his words but his ideas that were curious and original. He wished to arouse a mob, or if you will a rabble, to support those ideas; but not to support any ideas – least of all to support any ideas that they might happen to have already. Fundamentally and almost unconsciously he was indeed appealing to popular instincts that were not only equally fundamental but equally unconscious. But in the mere form and method of his utterance, he was much more disposed to ram information down their throats than to take hints from their faces. If he was in his way demagogic, he was much more definitely didactic. Education was an enthusiasm with him: from teaching economics as he taught French by a sort of public correspondence, to helping his own little boy with a horn-book. But while he was in private the very gentlest of teachers, he was in public, when talking to a crowd of farmers instead of to a little boy, the most violent and even offensive; to the child he was rather persuasive than didactic, and to the men not so much didactic as dictatorial.

We have already noted something of the sort about the English Grammar. He was a logician as well as a grammarian. He was the last man in the world to be really a pedant. He would always have preferred splitting infinitives to splitting straws. These criticisms of diction are also criticisms of thought; or of absence of thought. This was the period of which it used to be said, with all solemnity, that an English statesman never quite recovered from having uttered a false quantity in a Latin quotation in early life. It sounds like a parody on the secret sin of the mysterious baronet; but indeed he recovered easily enough from deserting the village maiden; and he never tried to recover from being drunk. Under these circumstances, Cobbett was surely justified in suggesting that too much notice was taken of a false quantity in

Latin, and too little of a false quality in English. To some it may seem a rather remote question whether the English statesman in talking Latin accented it right, considering that he almost certainly pronounced it wrong. But in any case Cobbett, if we may extend the metaphor, always threw the moral accent far back and let it fall on the root of the word. In that and many other respects he was really a Radical.

But our concern here is not so much with whether it was correct as with whether it was characteristic. Of course, if Cobbett had treated any abstract science it would have become a concrete science. If he had merely undertaken to set out the multiplication table it would have run: 'Twice one useless regiment is two useless regiments; twice two venal Ministers is four venal Ministers; twice three pluralistic parsonages is six pluralistic parsonages like those possessed by the Reverend Mr Hugg of Netherwallop,' and so on. If he had set out a system of astronomy, and had merely to give the names of the stars, he would have been unable to mention Mars without saying something caustic about Lord Wellington or Mercury, without a few contemporary illustrations of the connection between commerce and theft. No icy abstractions could freeze out that ferocious familiarity. It is said that the discoverer of the North Pole would see a Scotsman's cap on it; certainly the sight of that cap would fill Cobbett with sentiments sufficient to keep him warm. On that side the grammatical experiment illustrates only his obvious pugnacity; his tendency to personify everything in order to pelt it with personalities. But it illustrates something else as well. And it is exactly that something else that seems in a sense contrary, and yet is the completion of the character, without which it cannot be understood.

There was something cool about Cobbett, for all his fire; and that was his educational instinct, his love of alphabetical and objective teaching. He was a furious debater; but he was a mild and patient schoolmaster. His dogmatism left off where most dogmatism begins. He would always bully an equal; but he would never have bullied a pupil. Put a child before him to be taught arithmetic or the use of the globes, and he became in the most profound and even touching sense a different man. There came about him like a cold air out of the clean heavens, cooling his hot head, something that counted with him more than it does with most men; something about which we hear perhaps too much now as too little then; something that only too easily provides perorations for politicians or themes for ethical societies; but something which does exist in some men and did emphatically exist in this one. The pure passion of education went through him like a purging wind; he thirsted to tell young people about things – not about theories or parties or political allegations, but about things. Whether they were grammatical roots or vegetable roots or cube roots, he wanted to dig them up; to show them and to share them. He had the schoolmaster's enthusiasm for being followed, for being understood; his inmost ideal was a sort of white-hot lucidity. He above all men made the appeal: He that hath ears to hear, let him hear; though he was too prone to decorate with very long ears the rivals who would certainly refuse to hear. But the dunces were the dons. There was no dunce in the class he taught; for the whole fury of his genius was poured into simplifying his lesson to suit it to the village idiot.

For this reason also, and not only for the other, he had decorated his Grammar with grotesque caricatures. He was resolved to make English grammar amusing; and he did. It is not true that his only pleasure was in execrating somebody or even exposing something. Stronger even than these was his rational rapture in explaining something. He had learnt that in order to explain something it is necessary to hold the attention; and his examples always do hold the attention. In some ways, therefore, the two contrary forces in him come together, more than anywhere, in this strange volume; in what some would call this mad textbook.

But he appears as a better because a broader teacher in the Rural Rides. He really had a great talent for teaching; in the real sense in which a schoolmaster like a poet is born and not made. He could go back with the beginner to the beginnings. He could understand the pupil's failure to understand. He would take trouble to make everything mean something, and sift the language for terms to which other terms could be reduced. A model of educational method may be found in his little talk with the farmhand at Beaulieu Abbey. Most educated men, even of a didactic turn, would be content to tell the man that it was spelt Beaulieu but pronounced Buley, and leave the man merely puzzled. At best they would have told him that *Beau* is the French for fine and *lieu* the French for place; and left him with an arbitrary fact fallen out of the air, like the Hebrew word for hat or the Chinese word for umbrella. But Cobbett really translated the words, making them part of the man's own language. He pointed out that even in English we talk of a beau when we mean a buck or dandy; and talk of taking goods in lieu of money when we mean in place of money. There is not one educated man in a thousand who would think of those illustrations to make things clear to a yokel in a lane; and the man who habitually talked like that was one of the great schoolmasters of the world.

It is quite impossible to pick up all the varied and vivid trifles that are scattered through the *Rural Rides.* It would be undesirable even if it were not impossible. It would be saving the reader the trouble of reading the book; and it ought to be no trouble. The man who does not find one of Cobbett's books amusing is doomed to find every book dull. They contain a hundred fragments from which the whole habit of his life has been built up. They show him to us in a series of snapshots, in attitudes so active as to amount to the animation of a cinema. We can picture him swaggering about on his own farm at Botley, in the red waistcoat that he wore so appropriately, like a defiance to a whole herd of bulls. We can watch him peering over fences and hedges in his eager and shameless vanity, enquiring everywhere about Cobbett's Corn (the name he modestly gave to the maize he brought from America), and sternly admonishing those who were unconscious of their good luck in possessing it. We can behold him as he curses London from the hills; he always called it the Wen. But here again his humour is more subtle than it seems. We have noticed the same offhand offensiveness in his quotations in the English Grammar. With his artless artistry, he gives more weight to this abusive term by using it not so much abusively as allusively. Instead of saying, 'This vile city is only one monstrous Wen,' he is careful to say quite carelessly, 'I was coming from the Wen,' as if he were saying, 'I was coming from the Wood.' He seems to assume that everybody knows it by that name. It is impossible, I say, to deal with all these details; we can only pick out one or two because they are symbolic and consider the social view they symbolise.

For instance, we can see that even as a reactionary he was a realist. An excellent example of Cobbett's general attitude may be found in his view of fairs and markets. This is especially true in that his attitude is emphatically not what most of his critics and some of his supporters would suppose. On the theory that he was a sort of retrospective rustic, merely regretting the good old times, it would be easy enough to make a picture of such a sentimental veteran recalling the romance of his youth at fair and market. But Cobbett is really concerned with the business of the market, and not merely with the fun of the fair. He does not imagine that village maidens pass their whole lives dancing round the Maypole. Some of the later romantics of Young England would have been quite capable of making them set up a Maypole at Christmas, perhaps with a Christmas pudding on top of it. He does not even cling to that yet nobler pillar of Christendom, the greasy-pole with a leg of mutton on top of it; more truly Christian because offering more opportunities for a cheerful humility. He does not see it as an old world pageant, in the manner of Ruskin or William Morris. He sees it as an economic question as strictly as Ricardo or John Stuart Mill. Only, rightly or wrongly, he turns the economic argument the other way. It is also quite typical of him that his economics are really economical. He does not primarily praise the fair as a place in which people can spend money. He actually praises it as a way in which they can save money. And his argument, whether we agree with it or not, is perfectly practical and prosaic. I do not mean, of course, that he would not sympathise with the Maypole and the greasy pole; for he certainly would. I do not mean that he would not enjoy the enjoyment, for he certainly did. He had a pretty taste in pretty girls, as have many men who are quite happy with their own wives; he would certainly have liked to see them dancing round a Maypole; though perhaps he would not have been sufficiently modern and advanced to enjoy seeing one of them asserting sex equality and making her own career by climbing the greasy pole. He would have entirely sympathised with the girl whose lover lingered at the fair, when he had promised to buy her a bunch of blue ribbons, as it says in the song, to tie up her bonny brown hair. Perhaps, again, he would have been so old-fashioned as to doubt whether the girl would gain very much by never buying ribbon for her hair, but only ribbon for her typewriter. But all this was a matter of light sentiment with him; and he was quite sane enough to take his sentiment lightly. The basis of his argument was in no sense sentimental; it was perfectly practical as far as it went. It was that the young man would not have to pay so much for ribbons for the young woman, because the person selling the ribbons would not have to pay so much for building or renting a shop. Somebody somewhere else, he argued, living in an ordinary cottage and garden, would make the ribbons at home, as the old country lace makers made lace, and would then walk into the nearest market town and sell them to the young man, who had also walked into the same market town to buy them. The young woman would get her ribbons, and the young man would have so much more left to go towards Cottage Economy and the expenses of married life, which do not consist entirely of the purchase of ribbons. But suppose (Cobbett's argument ran) the cottage woman, instead of working in her own cottage in her own way, had to go to a special place for working, all the expenses of that place must be thrown in. Suppose the cottage woman has to come into the market and put up four walls and a roof in order to sell a ribbon. The expenses of the shop are also added to the expenses of the ribbon; and the young woman has fewer ribbons or (more probably) less housekeeping money. I am not now arguing whether this economic argument is sound. I am only pointing out that this economic argument is economic. Cobbett seldom felt comfortable unless his strongest sentimental instincts had some such solid foundation. I think on the whole the argument is quite sound as far as it goes; and it goes a good way, until we come into the world of such very large and very lifeless mass production that things can be produced cheaply, especially by huge and rich monopolies by which they can even be, for some time, produced at a loss. In other words, it probably is true that one big millionaire might own one big machine with wheels incessantly going round and reeling off interminable lengths of the same very ugly ribbon; and that he might even sell it below cost price for the pleasure of driving every other sort of better and more varied ribbon out of the market. But some (including the present writer) do not like monopolies of that kind or machines of that kind, or millionaires of that kind, or even ribbons of that kind; and some of us even decline under any circumstances to use them to tie up our bonny brown hair. In any case, in this sketch we are concerned less with controversy than with character; and it is essential to the character of Cobbett that he believed that a market was better than a shop, not merely because it was brighter or quainter or more picturesque, but because he thought it was cheaper. It must be noted as marking him off from the romantic reactionary, and even from the school of Ruskin when it denounced the economical tendency of economics. We can all sympathise with what Ruskin meant by the Lamp of Sacrifice. Even Cobbett could have sympathised, as his love of the great Gothic churches had shown; but if he had been arranging such an allegorical illumination, he would probably have added a Lamp of Thrift.

In this limited and definite sense he did object to England being a nation of shopkeepers. Today, of course, England is most unmistakably not a nation of shopkeepers. I myself, in a moment of controversial exaggeration, described it as a nation of shop walkers. But anyhow, it is obvious that the process which Cobbett condemned has not only gone far beyond anything that he described, but has gone far enough to destroy itself, as a thing covered by that description. If ownership be the test, it has been a process and a period of people losing things and not gaining them. It has been a process of people going into service, in the language of servants, into service if not into servitude. It has been a process of people losing even the little booth at the fair, that was thought so poor a substitute for the little farm in the fields. Somewhat sadly we can now toss away from us the taunt of our great enemy. By the best proof of all, the English are not a nation of shopkeepers. They have not kept their shops.

But the point here is that Cobbett was not weeping over lost causes; he was rather if anything raving over lost cash: or at any rate lost capital. He was perfectly practical; but he was sorry that the small capitalists were being ruined; and in the long run he may possibly turn out to be right. As we have said, he was emphatically not a mere *laudator temporis acti*. He was not merely crying over spilt milk; he was crying for justice over stolen cows. But he was not reckless in the sense of a friend to recklessness: on the contrary, he felt that such a licence to theft was the end of thrift. He gave his enemies beans, as the saying is, but he knew how many beans make five: and even counted them carefully.

It is curious that men of the type of Brougham were always lecturing the poor on foresight, when the one thing they could not do was to foresee the future of the poor. They were always urging them to thrift and urging them to set up a system which would make it impossible to be thrifty. Those who used the word thrift twenty times a day never looked at the word once. If they had, they would have seen that thrift depends upon thriving. In Shakespeare, it is used as practically meaning property or wealth; 'where thrift may follow fawning.' Unfortunately, in a modern plutocracy it can only follow fawning. It certainly cannot follow saving. A servant who is agreeably servile may possibly have a fortune by favouritism. But by no possibility could he save enough out of common wages to buy a farm, still less a shop in the town where land is priceless; and those are the sort of things for which men save. But it is the paradox of the whole position that the Utilitarians who were always preaching prudence committed this country to one of the most really reckless revolutions in history – the industrial revolution. They destroyed agriculture and turned England into a workshop; a workshop in which the workers were liable at any moment to be locked up and left to eat hammers and saws. The Radicals who did that were as picturesque as pirates, so far as pirates become specially picturesque when they burn their boats. In truth they were not so much metaphorically burning their boats: they were almost literally burning their barns. But there is something fitting in the accident by which the term Free Trader used to mean a smuggler. If romantic recklessness be the test, Cobden and Bright should always have appeared brandishing cutlasses and with a belt full of pistols.

But Cobbett did really value foresight; Cobbett did really believe in forethought; Cobbett did really believe in thrift. He was ever ready to urge a wise economy of expenditure with the wildest extravagance of words. He praised prudence in a series of the most appallingly imprudent speeches ever made by man. He howled and bellowed all the beauties of a sober and sensible and quiet life. But he was perfectly sincere; and it was really thrift and forethought and sobriety that he recommended. Only, it was the trouble with his forethought that it was, among other things, thought; and of his foresight that he could see a little further. He could see a little further than his nose; or that supercilious nose on which the spectacles of the economist were balanced. He saw that even when the economists were right in recommending economy, they were recommending it to people who could not possibly be economical. He saw that the economists were not even creating their own monster of an Economic Man; they were creating nothing but the thriftless thousands of a wandering proletariat. As for the ordinary Whigs and champions of Reform, he did not believe they were even trying to create anything except salaries and sinecures for themselves.

Then again, his coarseness is not only touched by shrewdness but by tenderness; of a sort much too shrewd to be sentimental. His charity was not cheap. To say that he had a sense of human equality will convey little to those who can make no sense of that sense. Perhaps it would be more intelligible to say that there are some who sympathise with the poor from the outside and some who can sympathise from the inside. There is one kind of man who pities a beggar because the beggar is so different from himself, and another who does it because the beggar is so similar. Many a perfectly sincere reformer will say, 'Imagine a man starving in such a slum,' as he would say, 'Imagine a man being really boiled by cannibals in a pot,' or, 'Imagine that a man really was chopped in pieces by Chinese torturers.' His phrase is a piece of perfectly honest rhetoric; but he knows that we do not really imagine it. But when Cobbett writes about it, we do imagine it. He does not deal in lurid description; in this matter he is rather unusually responsible and reasonable. He simply has the knack of making the thing happen to himself and therefore to his reader. There is an excellent illustration of his quieter method in one passage in the *Rural Rides*. He describes, in that plain and almost naked narrative style that seems to lie like strong morning daylight upon every detail of the day, how he started out riding with his son at dawn; how some hitch occurred about the inn at which he had intended to breakfast, and he rode on hoping to reach another hostelry in reasonable time; how other hitches occurred which annoyed him, making him scold the boy for some small blunders about the strapping of a bag; and how he awoke at last to a sort of wonder as to why he should be so irritable with a child whom he loved so much. And then it dawned upon him that it was for the very simple reason that he had had no breakfast. He, who had fed well the night before and intended to feed well again, who was well clothed and well mounted, could not deny that a good appetite might gradually turn into a bad temper. And then, with one of his dramatic turns or gestures, he suddenly summons up before us all the army of Englishmen who had no hope of having any breakfast until they could somehow beg work from hard or indifferent men; who wandered about the world in a normal state of hunger and anger and blank despair about the future; who were exposed to every insult and impotent under every wrong; and who were expected by the politicians and the papers to be perfectly mild and moderate in their language, perfectly loyal and law-abiding in their sentiments, to invoke blessings on all who were more fortunate and respectfully touch their hats to anybody who had a little more money.

Now, the unconscious ingenuity of that approach is that it surprises us from the inside. The man writing it has not struck any attitudes of a demagogue or a prophet of woe; he has not set out to describe slums as a missionary to describe savages. The man reading it does not know what is coming; but when it comes it comes to *him* and not to some remote stranger. It is he that feels the sinking within him that comes from the withdrawal of all our bodily supports; it is his own stomach that is hollow and his own heart that is sick with hope deferred. It will be all the better for him if it is his own brain that grows black and his own tongue bitter; if it teaches him for a moment what it must be to be a tramp walking with pain and bludgeoned by perpetual snubs and sneers and refusals. When a man has imagined that for a moment for himself, he knows for the first time what is meant by saying that men are brothers, and not merely poor relations. That is the psychological experience corresponding to the philosophical doctrine which for many remains a mystery: the equality of man.

It must also always be remembered, if we are to make any meaning of the tale, that it was this type of the very poor man, the tramp or the beggar, whom Cobbett almost unconsciously made the test of the time. He was not the man for whom it was possible to represent it as a good time. He was not the man who was being tolerated by toleration acts or enfranchised by reform bills. He was not the man who was being educated by Brougham's popular science or equipped by Arkwright's mechanical discoveries. He was not one of those whom the new world was making richer. As Cobbett would have put it in his bitter way, he had not the advantage of being a Jew who blasphemed Christ or a Quaker who ran away from patriotism. He was only a normal national baptized Englishman with nothing to eat. He was only a poor man; and he was quite certainly growing poorer.

Tyranny varies with temperament, especially national temperament. Some have taxed the poor, and some have enslaved the poor, and a few have massacred the poor; but the English rulers simply forgot the poor. They talked as if they did not exist; they generalised as if no such people need be included in the generalisation. They drew up reports of progress and prosperity in which the common people did not figure at all. They did not suppress the subject; by that time they simply did not think of it any more than a man shooting pheasants prides himself on killing flies or an angler counts the midges. It was said that the English founded an empire in a fit of absence of mind. It must be somewhat sadly added that they neglected a nation with the same absence of mind. Oligarchies far harsher and more arbitrary in legal form would probably have more responsibility in the sense of remembrance. A Roman official might have written in a famine, 'There is still food enough for the citizens and even the slaves.' A Victorian gentleman in the Hungry Forties simply sat down at his groaning mahogany and said, 'There is enough food.' A planter in South Carolina might well have been heard saying, 'The Blockade is starving the blacks as well as ourselves.' The merchant in Manchester was only heard saying, 'There may be a slump; but with the next boom we shall completely recover ourselves.' That is the mental blank peculiar to this mentality. They did not even look down with scorn and say, 'We are all comfortable, even if these vagabonds are beggared by their own vices.' They looked round with complete satisfaction and said, 'We are all comfortable.'

This distinction is simply a fact, and should not be mixed up with moral or sentimental recriminations. It is a character of the condition called capitalism, whether we dwell on the economic dependence or the political independence of the worker under capitalism. In part, doubtless, the proletarian was forgotten because he was free. The slave was remembered because he was always under the eye of the master. But I am not now arguing about whether nineteenth-century capitalism has been better or worse than slavery. I am

73

pointing out that the whole business of hiring men and sacking men did allow of forgetting men. It allowed of it much more than the servile system of owning men. Capitalism has produced a peculiar thing, which may be called oppression by oblivion. And this negative and indirect injustice was native both to what is good and what is bad in the English temper. It is the paradox of the English that they are always being cruel through an aversion to cruelty. They dislike quite sincerely the sight of pain, and therefore shut their eyes to it; and it was not unnatural that they should prefer a system in which men were starved in slums but not scourged in slave-compounds.

Now, here again we have one of the subtleties under the superficial simplicities of *Rural Rides*. Cobbett, it has been often repeated, was as English as any Englishman who ever lived. He had all the English virtues: the love of loafing and of lonely adventure; the spirit of the genial eccentric; the capacity to be a hermit without being a misanthrope; the love of landscape and of roads astray; and above all, that love of the grotesque that is as brave as a broad grin. Nor, as we say, was he without that softer side, only that with him it was generally the inside. I mean that it was in his private and domestic character that we see the English aversion to what is painful and severe. He was a very gentle father and schoolmaster, not only in practice but in theory; and much that he wrote on education almost anticipates the complete amnesty of the Montessori school. He always expressed himself strongly about the stupidity of schoolmasters knocking children about, though he did it with a cheerful readiness to knock the schoolmasters about. Here he does indeed touch something in the English that is behind their dislike of a scene. Victor Hugo in his *Art of being a Grandfather* describes in his rather boastful fashion how he had lashed the world like Isaiah or Juvenal, and refused to descend to the bathos of slapping a child. Cobbett had lashed the world like nobody in the world but Cobbett. And he had a better right than Hugo to say truly of himself that 'thunder should be mild at home.'

But when all this element in the great Englishman has been allowed for, it is still true that there was one quality in him that was not English. He was extremely provocative. He was as provocative as an Irishman. He refused to leave people alone. He refused emphatically to let sleeping dogs lie. It is not surprising that at the end he had the whole pack in full cry after him; and that it only gave him a further opportunity for turning on them and telling them they were all curs and mongrels, not to mention mad dogs. He always trailed his coat, especially so as to make men say that he had turned his coat. He rejoiced and exulted in a scene. There is nothing more vivid than that scene on which Mr Edward Thomas touched with great felicity, the great meeting which Cobbett had worked up to the point of a passionate enthusiasm for throwing him out. 'I stood up,' he says, 'that they might see the man they had to throw out.' That phrase is a photograph before the days of photography;

the picture of that big, snorting, bellicose farmer, standing up with distended nostrils and the expression which in the prize ring is called being a glutton.

Now, the combination in Cobbett of the deepest English humours and the love and understanding of England with this quality which is rare in England, the aggressive and challenging quality, is a sort of coincidence or contradiction which gave him his whole value in our politics and history. It was exactly because he was English in everything else, and not English in this, that he did serve England, and very nearly saved England. He very nearly saved her from that oppression by oblivion, that absent-minded cruelty of the mere capitalist, which has now brought upon her such accumulated and appalling problems in the industrial world. He was capable of being candid about cruelty; and indeed of being cruel about cruelty. He would not let sleeping dogs lie; he also would not let progressive politicians lie. While a rather oily optimism was being applied like oil, he rubbed in his pessimism like pepper. To a society that was more and more covering itself up with its own superficial success, he was always deliberately digging up the mass of submerged failure. To use a metaphor that would have appealed to him, he was always refusing to judge our society by the top layer of apples or strawberries in the basket, and always declaring that the shopkeeper was a swindler and the fruit underneath was rotten. While the whole of that version of things afterwards called Victorian was gently pressing everybody to judge England by an idealised version of the public schoolboy and the gentleman, he delighted to pester our very imagination with beggars and tramps. While the New Poor Law was putting away such people in prisons and police institutions, he delighted to exhibit them with all their sores like the cripples on the steps of a church in Italy.

But though in this he was an exception among Englishmen, he was still an English exception among Englishmen. The distinction should be understood; somewhat in the same sense, in spite of what is said to the contrary, a man like Parnell was an exception among Irishmen, but a purely Irish exception. Cobbett represented one piece of England awake where much of England was asleep: he represented certain English things in revolt that are commonly in repose. But his way of reaching even these was very national; since it was very casual and almost entirely experimental. He did not start with theories but with things; with the things he saw. A philosophy can be deduced from his comments; but we do not feel that they were deduced from a philosophy.

Lastly, he embodied the English paradox: because he was a sort of poet whose ideal was prose. He was easily infuriated; and he would have been immensely infuriated at being called a poet; or, still more, being called a mystic. But there was much more poetry in him than he knew. There was even much more mysticism in him than he knew; for a simple man is a mystery to himself. And nothing is more notable in the great panorama of the *Rural Rides* than the fact that he often sees things in an epical and symbolical fashion which others saw in a very material or mechanical fashion. To take only one instance: all the books and speeches and pamphlets of the latter period of his life are full of allusions to Old Sarum. It was, of course, the outstanding, not to say outrageous example of the anomalies of the unreformed representative system; a place that had practically ceased to exist without ceasing to send legislators to make laws for England. There are any number of jokes and anecdotes and debates and diatribes about Old Sarum; but they are all concerned with it as something on a map or even in a table of figures. The joke is an abstract and arithmetical joke. The idea of anybody *going* to Old Sarum would seem somehow like going to the Other End of Nowhere. It is intensely characteristic of Cobbett that for him alone Old Sarum was a place; and because it happened to be a high and hilly place, it stood up in his imagination with the monstrosity of a mountain. He called it the Accursed Hill. That single title, compared with the terms used by pamphleteers and politicians, has in it something of the palpable apocalypse. We can fancy him seeing it afar off from some terrace of hills looking over the coloured counties, as some primitive traveller might have fancied he saw afar off the peak of Purgatory, or the volcanic prison of the Titans. He hated it not as arithmetical anomalies can be hated; but as places can be hated, which is almost as persons can be hated. And in all this, as compared with the contemporary rationalism, there was more mysticism precisely because there was more materialism. There is almost in such a combination a sort of sacrament of hate. His feeling about the sin and shame of Sarum was of the same moral type as the feeling about the sanctity of the other Sarum, which might have been felt by some ardent devotee of the Use of Sarum. But in that sense Cobbett could not see the use of Sarum.

This imaginative quality in the man is all the more interesting because it is partly unconscious and partly suppressed. In so far as he had an imaginative concept of himself, we might almost say it was the concept of not being imaginative. Even the world which has understood him so little has at least understood that he was essentially and emphatically English. But perhaps the most English thing about him was that he contrived by sheer poetry to picture himself as prosaic. He was so imaginative that he imagined himself to be merely a plain man. This is really an illusion that explains much of the history of John Bull; as indeed it explains the whole legend and ideal of John Bull. As poets dream not of a poet but of a hero, so a nation of poets has called up as its ideal the vision of a practical man. But in Cobbett's time, and especially in Cobbett's case, what there was of illusion in this was quite innocent; and he did not know that there was anything spiritual or elemental about him. That universe that exists in the brain of every man was then rather by way of being a buried universe; and those were few who, like Blake and Swedenborg, dived after its submerged stars. In the Age of Reason there was some tendency for the soul to become the subconsciousness. Cobbett certainly was cheerfully unconscious of having any subconsciousness. I shudder to think what would have happened to anybody who had told him he had a complex; and indeed there was very little complex about him. In that sense he believed in reason as rigidly as Tom Paine; and the world in which he moves over downland and dale and country town is eternally in the broad daylight. But there is one passage in that practical pilgrimage in which we do get a glimpse of those deeper things, at once more dark and more illuminated. It is all the more moving because it comes quite without warning in the middle of that quiet and unpretentious narrative, and with one turn takes on the character of some terrible allegory. There is something about it mysterious and macabre, like a dark woodcut of Albert Dürer.

He describes how he came in his careful wanderings to a district in which the large estates had been reorganised by new landlords of a certain kind: landlords named Ricardo and Baring and other rather foreign and financial names, whom he was wont to name very frankly. All day his heart had grown heavier with the increasing sense that the country was passing into the hands of these oriental merchants, and he was probably brooding, as he often did, on the very darkest version of their history and character, when he saw a strange object or ornament or accident standing up in those smooth and well-ordered grounds neatly fenced from the road. It was actually in the shape of a cross; 'big enough and broad enough to crucify a man on.' With something that makes his staccato style sound for the first time like broken speech, he repeats more than once, 'Aye, big enough and broad enough to crucify a man on.' And then he says that his horse, who was accustomed to the ambling trot with which he rambled about for his adventures, was startled by the spur or the gesture which urged him to sudden activity. He must have gone, he says, at a great and very uncommon pace as he got away from that place. 'I think he [meaning the horse] must often have wondered what gave me wings that once and that once only.'

That curious incident is all the more impressive because Cobbett tells it with powerful restraint and saying as little as may be of its emotional side. He who flung fierce words about like a fury slinging flame, always had a rather fine instinct of sobriety and simplicity when it came to the few things, rather in the background of his mind, which he did really though vaguely reverence. But in this case something rather more unusual and even uncanny was involved. A man has been pottering about from farm to farm and town to town on a trotting horse, inspecting crops, making notes about wages, cocking an eye at the weather and calling for a glass of ale at the inn; but all with the sense that this older England is passing away, and feeling it more and more as he comes nearer to Surrey and the suburbs, or to the great new estates run by the new gentry. Their names are strange names; and he has suspicions that even those names are not always their own. Their faces are strange faces; associated in his mind with sketches of eastern travel or with pictures in the family Bible. They are very busy; very orderly; in their own way very philanthropic. But what are they doing, what are they driving at, what is the ultimate design by which they build? There lies like a load upon him the impression that the whole world is being reformed; and it is being reformed wrong. The world's great age begins anew; and it begins wrong. He cannot think where it will all end; what form so foreign and perhaps formless a growth is ultimately meant to take. And then he sees, standing up quite neat and new and solid in the sunlight, something that seems crude and freshly carpentered and yet frightfully familiar; not a symbol but rather a substantial purpose; not an emblem but an end. And we know not what shock of revelation or revulsion all but unhorsed that strong rider as on the road to Damascus; something indescribable, overwhelming a plain man in a passion of subtleties, that has no outlet but a rush of flight; and far away down the darkling English lanes the throb and thunder of the flying hooves. For that unholy cross the heathen saw stood up still ugly and unsanctified; black against the daybreak of the world, the shape of shame; and saving such a strange flash of reversion, the cross no Christian will ever see.

VII

LAST DAYS AND DEATH

A mere outline of the career of Cobbett has been broken or interrupted here for the sake of two studies of his literary personality. That outline left him in England after his second return from the United States. The time of his return was largely the time of his triumph in spite of, or rather because of, the tumultuous hour in which he returned. In this period he received all the highest compliments which he was ever likely to receive. He was hailed as a democratic deliverer, not only by his own natural following among the farm-labourers of the southern shires, but by the grim and growing power of the Trades Unions of the Midlands and the North. He was given a great public banquet and toasted with tremendous enthusiasm. He was invited, in many times and places during these later years, to stand for Parliament. He was eventually elected to Parliament. If the Reform Government had really been a Reform Government, he might have been a Minister in it or received any honour that popular government could bestow. In any case he received, in this his time of honour, the highest of all these honours. He was prosecuted by the Government for sedition.

But the man in the dock was a very different person from the dazed and disillusioned Tory farmer who had once stood distracted between the doom hanging over his farm and the doom hanging over his country. He stood in the dock like a man risen from the dead. He was an incarnate and historic revenge that had renewed its youth like the eagle's. He was far younger than when he was young. If it was foolish of the politicians to have prosecuted him on the first occasion, there is something of the madness that marks the wrath of the gods in their repetition of the folly so long afterwards. They were actually silly enough to attempt to make him responsible for the Luddites smashing the machines. He had not, of course, the smallest difficulty in showing that he had actually written to the Luddites asking them not to smash the machines. He could and did call Brougham as a witness to prove that his appeal had actually been used on the side of law and order. But Cobbett was not likely to confine himself to the defensive, with such an opening for a counter-offensive. He tore to rags their ridiculous case against him; then he drew a deep breath into his great lungs, and they heard his case against them. He let himself go; we might say he let himself loose. Tribunals and officials had a startling experience of what sort of elemental rage had been dwelling among them. He browbeat the browbeating judges; he bullied the bullies of the bar; he raised the jury against them like a mob; it was the hour of his life. For once at least he could make men understand that he did well to be angry; and he did. He spat out his passionate contempt for all that cold and cowardly world which had gone about to trap him lest he should somewhere let out the truth. He gave its own name to all that bottomless baseness in the comfortable classes, that would destroy a man for his sympathy with the poor. He swept away all the ridiculous relevancies of whether he had said this or that about an election or a trade union, and attacked the thing his enemies were really attacking. He accused them of their accusation. He charged them with charging a man with having a heart for the oppressed. He told them why they hated him; and showed them the face of their own fear. It was not because he was blatant or inconsistent or coarse or reckless; even if he was. It was not because he raged or ranted or made a noise. It was because of those silent on whose behalf he made a noise; of the dumb for whom he ranted and the impotent for whom he raged. It was his love of the poor that made him horrible to his enemies; and in that hour he made them feed on the full horrors that such love reveals. When he had done shaking the court of justice with his voice, everything around him seemed shrunken and silent; the jury acquitted him almost mechanically, and he left the court, if not without a stain on his character, at least with a smile on his face broader than the grim smile he wore during his sentence to Newgate. He might have been dismounting after a holiday ride along the hills, before an honest alehouse of his youth. And indeed he had been doing the same thing; he had been enjoying himself.

That hour in the dock was the supreme moment of his life; and though in one sense it was followed by more success and popularity than he had hitherto, he was never again so near to his own vision of triumph. He became more and more identified with the great movement against the rotten boroughs, which culminated (or collapsed) with the great Act of 1830. The Reform movement united him with many who had once been his friends and with many who would always have been his enemies. But the Reform movement was very different from the Reform Bill. Cobbett lived to see

Reform, but not the Reform he had longed to see. He sat in Parliament, but not in the Parliament where he wished to sit. The atmosphere he hated most of all, more than any smoke of destruction or any smell of decay, the Whig atmosphere, was what prevailed in the new Parliament and the new Ministry. If he watched with too harsh a sneer its first act of emancipating the niggers by an enormous bribe to the nigger-drivers, we may imagine (or fail to imagine) how he regarded its second act, which was to complete and extend the most cruel Tudor policy against poor vagabonds, by passing the New Poor Law and putting them into prisons called workhouses. To a more detached mind there might seem something of symmetry and balance in thus simultaneously letting out black people and locking up white.

Before this had happened, of course, and while it was happening, he had pursued his other controversial interests, and figured in several other fields. He had taken a seed farm in Kensington where he conducted an experiment in bartering goods for labour, and sold all sorts of things. His *Register* still sold like hot cakes; the cakes continued to be very hot indeed. Some of them were more than most people could swallow, in the way of absolute assertions, positive prophecies, and personal threats. He was by this time a great public character; from some points of view a great comic character. It is possible that some people tried to take a rise out of him. Sometimes the laugh was on his side; sometimes on the other. But this could always be said of him, that he stood in the same swaggering attitude whether he stood alone or backed by a whole nation. Two examples will serve: of the former, the joke about the gridiron; of the latter, an affair that had happened earlier – that of the Royal Divorce.

Certainly Cobbett had a way of brazening things out, whether we think him right or wrong; indeed, we cannot but feel a sort of breathless admiration especially when we think him wrong. The story of the gridiron which he came to carry like a coat-of-arms is an excellent illustration of his invincible impudence. It arose out of a trifle, or at any rate out of a detail; a detail which was very doubtful and not at all decisive. The Government had declared, in connection with the crisis which necessitated paper money, that things would improve, and that certain payments would be made in coin. Cobbett, contradicting flatly and flying into a passion, as was his habit about a hundred things large and small, had said he would be broiled on a gridiron if the Government could do any such thing. It was of course only one of his characteristic idioms; which were at once homely and extravagant. He meant no more by this singular fireside fantasy than he would have meant by using the more familiar theological fantasy and saying he would see them damned first. Indeed, he would have looked forward to seeing the Ministers damned with a much more solemn and religious expectation. It only illustrates in passing a certain individual twist that he could always give to his plain talk, that where another man would say 'I'll be hanged if you do,' or possibly 'I'll be shot if you do,' he had the fine fastidiousness to say 'I'll be broiled if you do.' But when his enemies began to shoot this light thing at him as an arrow from his own quiver, he wore it like a feather in his cap. He seized the opportunity of solidifying into an emblem something that had been but an idle word. They taunted him by turning his metaphor against him; and he answered them by turning their taunt against them. He hung up a huge gridiron outside his house; he brandished his gridiron in controversy like a club in a street riot. It seemed impossible to believe that any man could be wrong on a point that he pressed so provocatively; it was manifest that no man could be ashamed of an episode which he so paraded and perpetuated. And yet, in the actual episode itself, it is quite possible that he was quite wrong. A slight financial recovery of that sort was certainly not so insanely impossible as his metaphor implied; and as a matter of fact he was wrong in his general notion that *immediate* failure would follow the new financial experiments. Anyhow, he would probably have behaved in exactly the same way whatever had happened in the particular matter of which he originally spoke. It may be disputed whether this audacity should be classed as one of his vices or merely one of his talents. But certainly he had this talent, or if you will this trick, of turning defeat into victory. In this sense it is true to say that he had the tricks of a demagogue. Only, something more in the way of a definition of demagogy is needed before justice is done to him. But he did shout down his hecklers; and it was he on the hustings, much more than Johnson at the tea table, who knocked men down with the butt-end when his pistol missed fire. And he did have the power of making his very digressions and irrelevancies more important than other men's questions; the great gridiron did brand itself on men's memory when its origin was forgotten, and glowed through the twilight of time almost like the sacred gridiron of St Lawrence.

It was characteristic of Cobbett's instinct for the national sentiment, for a sort of sporting variety of chivalry very deep in his people, that he had thrown himself with refreshing fury against the opponents of Queen Caroline. It is also characteristic of his fighting spirit that he must have been rather more of a nuisance to her supporters than to her enemies. He bullied and browbeat the Queen's lawyers and advisers, he came near to bullying and browbeating the Queen; but in the main he respectfully confined himself to pestering and plaguing her. Yet his aim, as was often the case with him, was none the less sane because it was strenuous. It was his whole purpose to pin her to her full claims, and especially to nail her to her post in London, when there was any danger of her leaving the country; which might look like a surrender. So Dundee, a man of the fighting sort, had tried to nail James the Second, and prevent him seeming to abandon his claim with his country. Perhaps the feeling was the fiercer because Cobbett's old enemy Brougham was the lady's chief legal adviser; and nothing pleased Cobbett so much as to suggest that he was too legal to be loyal. Anyhow, there is no doubt that Cobbett was quite sincerely loyal. He enjoyed, indeed, not without an innocent vanity, his chivalric attitude as the champion of a woman; he had all his life a very honourable simplicity in his view of women. There are some very delightful touches in the letters of his daughter, who adored him, but who does not conceal her amusement at papa's new grandeur and gratification in his powdered hair and new court-suit and sword. There was no red waistcoat on these occasions.

The affair of Caroline of Anspach need not be fully discussed here; though it is not without interest and certainly not without irony. The irony most relevant to her relations with the great demagogue is its suggestion of something not uncommon in democratic emotions. The mob has a curious way of being right by being wrong. It often champions the wrong person to punish the right person. It supports a true view by a false argument; or convicts a real criminal of an unreal crime. It may be doubted whether the official wife of George the Fourth deserved all the democratic devotion that was poured out for her; but there is little doubt that George the Fourth by this time deserved most of the democratic detestation that was hurled against him. Yet he had once been a far more generous and even a far more liberal man. And the sin that had rotted his honour was not his repudiation of his official wife Caroline, but his repudiation of his real wife Mrs Fitzherbert. And it is the supreme irony of that strange story that his old and real crime rose from the grave against him, at the very moment when he was committing what was regarded as a more indefensible crime, but was really far more defensible. Lord Liverpool and the King's friends, goaded by the defiances of Cobbett and the mob, brought in a bill legally divorcing and degrading the Queen. The Queen's party retorted with a boldness that smacks very much of Cobbett's controversial spirit; they threatened to bring up the King's first and secret marriage as an illegality forfeiting his whole position, because it was a marriage to a Catholic. At this point also, not for the first time, England and the great English agitator touched for a moment the hidden thing that had remained behind English history; at first a martyr and always a witness, and perhaps at last a deliverer.

It is more difficult to make the people support the cause of the people than to make it support the cause of a person. Cobbett had not only the masses but most of the middle class with him about the dubious royal romance. He stood much more alone in dealing with the indubitable popular reality. That reality to which he testified with unwearied violence was something quite simple; yet it seemed to be too simple for the educated to understand. He shouted it in a place more and more padded and cushioned with a comfortable optimism; and it had no echo. He shouted it in such a fashion that many of his hearers would have retorted that it was well that he should be in a padded cell. Yet what he shouted is of a certain curious interest and is worth recording. It might be typified very tersely in what he said in answer to one of the leading statesmen, who said that we might look with confidence to the future, 'because all the great interests are prospering.' Cobbett wrote in large letters like a man scrawling on a great wall or the side of a hill: 'The working classes, then, are not a great interest.'

He added grimly that perhaps they might be some day. Those who see in Trade Union dictatorship a red dawn of revolutionary tyranny may pause upon the postscript: I am concerned to point out that this was, first and last, what he had to say: and he could not say it in the Reform Parliament. It is notable that a very fair sketch of Cobbett says that he did nothing in Parliament but make a crack-brained attack on Peel. Yet he can be judged even by what he attacked.

That Cobbett should have attacked Peel, especially in Parliament, is exactly what any understanding person would have expected; I am tempted to say what any understanding person would have hoped. It was equally obvious that he would attack him in Parliament in very unparliamentary language. It is most obvious of all that his attack would be utterly unintelligible to all the Parliamentarians who can only speak the Parliamentary language and are unacquainted with the English language. Peel was a model Parliamentarian; in other words, he was a monument of everything that Cobbett detested and despised. Peel was a Tory without traditions; Peel was a Liberal without popular sympathies. Peel was Parliament, and could not be expected to have the faintest notion of what the people felt or experienced. The only truly popular tradition about Peel has nothing to do with the inscriptions on the statues or the speeches on the Corn Laws. It is the tact that, far down in the depths of a democratic world that politicians never visit, the slang names for the new police were 'Bobbies' or 'Peelers.' And if we want to seize the very soul of Peel and his Parliamentary type, we can fix it in the fact that he organised a tremendously powerful and privileged *gendarmerie* for the control or coercion of the people, and thought they could be distinguished from the guards of Continental despots by the fact that they wore top-hats. That was the definition of Peelite citizenship: bribery in a top-hat; tyranny in a top-hat; anything so long as it was in a top-hat. All that is really to be called British hypocrisy, all that can be fairly classed as English snobbery, all the vices that grew under cover of decorum, and of which the very vulgarities were shy – all that is truly expressed in the fact that men in those days were set to control mobs in top-hats, just as they played cricket in top-hats. It is no contradiction to this that the hat has since evolved into a helmet. It might have evolved into a complete suit of armour, so long as it evolved; civilisation was the essence of that cautious and creeping philosophy. The point is that at the beginning the gendarme would not have been accepted if he had appeared in a cocked hat. It was a world, as Tennyson should have said, where tyranny slowly broadened down from precedent to precedent. The essential thing of the epoch was the thin end of the wedge. It is needless to ask what Cobbett thought of the thin end of the wedge; he who always fought with the thick end of the cudgel. Nothing – not even his defence of Factory Acts with the scornful phrase that his England depended on yeomen, but the new Lancashire was apparently lost without little girls – was so typical as the fact that he opposed a Police Force.

The short way of putting it is that Cobbett failed in Parliament. In a longer view it may be Parliament that failed. We can hardly say that the politicians failed to use the genius and energy of one of the greatest of Englishmen; for he was not a man to be used for any ends but his own, and they did not in the least desire to serve those ends. There was no possible point of contact, even for contradiction. It would be a very inadequate metaphor to say he was a fish out of water; for it was rather the politicians that were fishy. It would be truer to say that he was a very incautious diver drowning in a tank; but the truth is that he was simply a bull in a china shop. His sort of English, his sort of eloquence, his gesture, and his very bodily presence were not suitable in any case to senatorial deliberations. His was the sort of speaking that may make the welkin ring, but only makes the chairman ring a little bell. His attitude and action had about them the great spaces of the downs or the sweeping countrysides; the lifting of the great clouds and the silent upheaval of the hills. His warnings and rebukes sounded more homely and natural when they were shouted, as a man might shout across a meadow a rebuke to a trespasser or a warning against a bull. But that sort of shouting when it is shut up in a close and heated room has the appearance of madness. The company received the impression of a mere maniac. Yet there was not a man in that room who had a clearer head or a clearer style, or a better basis of common sense. And he showed easily enough in his English Grammar that it was really he who could reason and his critics who could only rant.

Indeed, a change was passing over England which he was already too old to understand; under the double rule of so patrician a Liberal as Melbourne and so bourgeois a Tory as Peel. An atmosphere was being generated not exactly like anything that had ever existed or perhaps will ever exist again; in which the jests of Canning would have been quite as inappropriate as the curses of Cobbett. It was not exactly a creed or a cause, or even a spirit; the nearest description is to say that it was a silence. All its undertakings were understandings; all its laws were unwritten laws. There was a silent understanding in the new middle class that it would not really rebel against the aristocracy. There was a silent understanding in the aristocracy that it would not really resist the invasion of the middle class. There was a silent alliance between the two that neither would really think about that third thing which moved in the depths visible for an instant in burning hayricks and broken machines. It was an understanding that produced its own courtesy and culture, its own poets and painters, its own patriotism and historic pride; so that we who were born in the last days of that tradition can never treat it altogether without piety and gratitude. The atmosphere had then no name; but a few years afterwards there was found for it a name and a figure and a national symbol; when a girl stood crowned before the altar at Westminster. We call it the Victorian Age.

It is not very likely that many members of Parliament noticed a little before this time that a seat in the House of Commons was empty. To a much greater extent than the profane vulgar are aware, the House of Commons often largely consists of empty seats. On important occasions, when there was more of a bustle and a crowd, the gap might be even less noticeable; there were so many serious things to hold the attention. There was the question of whether one Graham with the assistance of another Graham, his brother, could or could not have formed a Ministry that would include a gentleman named Grey. There was the question of whether somebody known as Lord Althorpe would soon be turned into somebody else called Earl Spencer. Under the strain of pressing problems of this kind, the Commons were not likely to trouble about the more and more frequent and eventually prolonged absence of one member or even of one vote; for indeed the vote had been as erratic as the member. His name was down in the lists among that queer and laughable little minority that had voted against the New Poor Law; along with Dan O'Connell and such odd creatures. Lately he had not been seen about at all. Probably nobody knew that in the last few days William Cobbett had gone back to his farm and died.

Far away on those great windy and grassy heights where he had gone crow-scaring as a child, his funeral procession trailed as black and meagre as a string of crows. They buried him in the little churchyard at Farnham; and he had died on the farm not far off that lay on the hillside looking across to the hill town of Guildford: a place of steep streets and a crown of roofs and spires which, seen from a distance, seems not unworthy of its noble medieval name. He had a happy death, who in the last achievement of his ambition had had an unhappy life. For he was suffered to die, after all his wanderings, among those he loved, and in the privacy which he loved to be the cover of such love, with all his appetite for a loud publicity in other things. Considering what a name he left, the privacy might have been called neglect; but in that sense, and especially in that mood, he would certainly have preferred to be to that extent neglected. Only his family and a few friends appear as recognisable figures in the landscape of his funeral; but as they carried the coffin through meadow and churchyard, there followed it one lonely figure that would have been conspicuous in any landscape; a man of giant stature, clad in black and with a white glove on his right hand: O'Connell.

It seems to have been the general impression of his contemporaries that he, who had survived hard riding and the sea and prison and the American summer, was eventually killed by the House of Commons. Chatham had carried his dramatic talent almost to the point of dying in the House of Lords. But certainly Westminster was the very last place where Cobbett would have wished to die – or for that matter to live. He had no such power of illusion as had enabled the great Imperialist to live and die in a passion of patriotic play-acting. Indeed, Cobbett had no power of illusion at all; that is why he was not what people call a practical man. That was especially why he could never manage to be a Whig; however much he might be called a Tory or a Radical. He could never have understood the sincerity there was in time self-deception of a man like Burke, who could look back on the oligarchical intrigues of 1688 and onwards in a glow of Constitutional enthusiasm. Perhaps to say that he was never a Whig is but another way of saying that he was not an aristocrat. History was not a hobby; politics were not a game, even a game played for money. He had that indefinable attitude which marks the man who has always had to earn his own living. He wanted history and politics to be useful; in that sense he was quite utilitarian. In the strict sense of the word, he was not a gentleman – he was a yeoman. He was a farmer who worked for a harvest; not a landscape painter or even a landscape gardener. All his wild life long he was working for a harvest; even when men thought he was sowing the wild oats of fanaticism; even when they thought he was sowing the dragon's teeth of revolution. He was trying to get results; and did not mind how hard he worked to get them. He worked to get a reform of Parliament; he worked to get a more popular control of Parliament: not because he particularly wanted to see the working of a new constitution in the abstract, but because he thought the old constitution was delaying the harvest. He worked for a right to take a hand in the work. He worked for a place among the new rulers of a new realm. He worked for a seat at Westminster because he really believed, more or less, that it would be a sort of throne from which he would see all England rejoicing in the new liberty since the hirelings and hacks of the wicked squires were gone and there had been summoned, in the ancient language of English liberty, a Free Parliament. The height from which he would look over that landscape of liberty would be higher than the Accursed Hill. He would see a New Sarum almost as ideal as the New Jerusalem, if not descending out of heaven from God, at least lifted towards heaven by the giant limbs of liberated man; by the proud toil and spontaneous prudence of the free. The new Parliament was meant to make a new people. And almost the first thing it did was to pass the New Poor Law. Almost the first thing it did was to hand over little Oliver Twist to be starved and beaten by Bumble and Claypole and sell English children into slavery for being poor.

There is an irony that is like an agony and is beyond speech or measure. It were vain to wonder, in the normal way, what manner of words would have come to those all too tempestuous lips; what lucid violence of logic as of light through rending rocks would have tried to do justice to that towering contradiction, in the days when the giant was young. Much he did say, of course, in his own way. But there was something in that final contradiction that could not so be contradicted finally or fully: and when Cobbett came with the clearer eyes of later life to look at the Reform Parliament, to look steadily at its Reformers and its Parliamentarians, to absorb the whole scene of how such laws are made and how such men make them; to sit in his seat in silence for a little, and take in all that enormous thing calmly and completely – then he made the only comment at all commensurate with it, or equal in eloquence to the occasion: he died.

The great world with its wheels of progress that went rolling over him did not understand his death any more than his life. A hundred years afterwards he is perhaps better known than he was ten years afterwards, or even ten minutes afterwards. Two hundred years afterwards, perhaps, he will be known better still. Johnson is more human and familiar to every casual reader today than he was to Churchill or Horace Walpole; but Johnson had a bodyguard of faithful friends who really understood him, his quaint weaknesses and his mighty worth. Cobbett hardly had a friend outside his family; and it is doubtful whether there had ever been one human being who really understood what he meant. His political allies were not friends; and they were not generally for very long allies. And the reason was that not one of them could enlarge his mind to understand the mind of Cobbett; or that immense desire for the deliverance and perpetuation of the whole huge humanity of England. The makers of the French Pantheon, wisely combining republican and royal and imperial trophies, have inscribed their common monument, 'To All the Glories of France.' If any man as wise had stood by the little gravestone in the churchyard of Farnham, he might have traced the words, 'To All the Glories of England.' All the other leaders were falling apart into foolish party systems and false antitheses; into Tories who were mere squires, and Radicals who were mere merchants. Windham had been his friend; but who could expect Windham to understand what he felt about the wild justice of the Luddite fires? Orator Hunt had been his ally; but who could expect Hunt to know what Cobbett was talking about when he praised the spires of the Gothic churches or the saints of the Dark Ages? This uneducated man was too well educated for all his contemporaries. He stood in a world which believed that it was broadening; and the whole mind of that world was narrower than his own. It believed itself to be growing modern and many-sided; and he alone saw that it was growing monomaniac and mean. And that larger vision died with him: and vanished for a hundred years.

Cobbett was only too ready to give people, in the language of the comic landlady, a piece of his mind. But the accidental phrase is after all an accurate phrase. It was only a piece of his mind that was ever given to anybody: a rather ragged piece often torn off in a rather random fashion: but not the whole truth that he really meant, for that he had great difficulty in giving to anybody, perhaps even to himself. Talkative as he was, it may be that he never said enough; and lucid as he was, it may be that he never quite got to the point. But the point was a whole point of view. And whether it was his fault or the other people's fault, that point of view was never really taken by anybody else: nobody stood exactly where he stood or saw the world exactly as he saw it; or others would have realised that, amid all his contradictory phrases and combative passions, he did in a real sense of his own see life steadily and see it whole. As we look back on his life, even the views that were not consistent with each other seem to be consistent with him. A friend would not deny that he contradicted himself; but a friend would be able to guess when and where he would probably contradict himself. Only in this sense it is true to say that he never had a friend. He had affections, and he had alliances; but not one true intellectual friendship.

There was this true distinction in the mind of the self-taught farmer: that his mind is a place where extremes meet. When it can be said of a man that the Tories thought him a Radical, and the Radicals thought him a Tory, the first thing that will occur to us is that he is a moderate. It can truly be said of Cobbett; and the very last thing that would occur to anybody would be to call him a moderate. He was not only the reverse of a moderate, he was something that would be utterly bewildering to any moderate. He was an extremist all round. He was more Tory than most Tories, and more Radical than most Radicals. In other words, it was because he was original; but it was also because he was universal. He did not altogether understand his own universality; and he expressed it mostly in the form of inconsistency. He was fanatical, but he was not narrow. With all his fanaticism, he was really looking at things from too many points of view at once to be understood by those who wore the blinkers of a party or even a theory. He seemed to be at all extremes, because he had in some sense encircled and surrounded his whole generation. Ignorant and violent as he seemed on the surface, his spirit was like one that had lived before and after. He was there before they were all born, in the crowded medieval churches. He was there after they were all dead, in the crowded congresses of the Trades Unions. It was not knowledge, but it was understanding, in the sense of sympathy. When we find this sort of universality we find, I think, a thing on the heroic scale. It would surely be no bad definition of greatness in a man, to say that we can strike out in any direction and still find the circumference of his mind.

There was never a Cobbettite except Cobbett. That gives him an absolute quality not without a sort of authority. He was a full man and a ready man, but he was not an exact man. He was not a scientific man or in the orderly and conscious sense even a philosophical man. But he was, by this rather determining test, a great man. He was large enough to be lonely. He had more inside him than he could easily find satisfied outside him. He meant more by what he said even than the other men who said it. He was one of the rare men to whom the truisms are truths. This union of different things in his thoughts was not sufficiently thought out; but it was a union. It was not a compromise; it was a man. That is what is meant by saying that it was also a great man. There was something in him that the world had not taught him; even if it was too vast and vague for him to teach it to the world. Things were part of that thing that could not be parts of any other thing. That is why he had no real intellectual friendships among the intellectuals of his day, when all allowance is made for his real faults of vanity and violence and readiness to quarrel. It is easy to argue about how he came to quarrel with his best friends. It is more penetrating to ask how he could ever come to agree with them. Even to the best of them his whole outlook, which seemed to him so simple, would have been bewildering. How was Orator Hunt to understand that the great empty churches with their gaping mouths cried aloud that they also belonged to the future, because they belonged to the past? How was the Right Honourable William Windham to understand that riotous artisans in the Black Country were also appealing to the past, as well as threatening the future? How was Mr Carlile the atheist bookseller to know that a ruined abbey and a raging mob were one thing; and that thing liberty? How was Lord Brougham to understand that a field of clover and a grotesque gridiron were one thing; and that thing England?

That is the paradox of Cobbett; that in a sense he quarrelled with everybody because he reconciled everything. From him, at least, so many men were divided, because in him so many things were unified. He appeared inconsistent enough in the thousand things that he reviled; but he would have appeared far more inconsistent in the things that he accepted. The breadth of his sympathy would have been stranger than all his antipathies; and his peace was more provocative than war. Therefore it is that our last impression of him is of a loneliness not wholly due to his hatreds, but partly also to his loves. For the desires of his intellect and imagination never met anything but thwarting and wounding in this world; and though the ordinary part of him was often happy enough, the superior part was never satisfied. He never came quite near enough to a religion that might have satisfied him. But with philosophies he would never have been satisfied, especially the mean and meagre philosophies of his day. The cause he felt within him was too mighty and multiform to have been fed with anything less than the Faith. Therefore it was that when he lay dying in his farmhouse on the hills, those he had loved best in his simple fashion were near to his heart; but of all the millions of the outer world there was none near to his mind, and all that he meant escaped and went its way, like a great wind that roars over the rolling downs.

This book began with an indefensible piece of personal recollection, and I fear it will have to end with another. Perhaps I might plead the influence of the man I have been studying and trying to understand; who has been called egotistical, though I should be content to call him autobiographical. As Mr Cole pointed out in his admirable biography, Cobbett treated his ego as an emblematic figure of England, as Whitman did his of America. My own memories can have no such symbolic excuse; but I passed much of my childhood along that main thoroughfare where Cobbett had his seed farm at Kensington; and one of the last things my own father told me was a tale of a strange object hanging above the road, before alterations and destructions removed it; one glimpse of a symbolic shape more ugly and ungainly than a gallows in the sunlight: the Gridiron.

All that he hated has triumphed on that spot. The ordinary shop that he thought a nuisance has swelled into the big emporium he would have thought a nightmare; the suburb has sunk deep into the new London; but the road still runs westward down which he went riding so often, heading for the open country, and leaving the Wen as far as possible behind. The Wen has pursued him, shooting out further and further in telescopic perspective, past Hammersmith and Chiswick and Richmond; and still I seem to see the back of that vanishing rider ever ahead, and lessening amid changing scenery; hills turning about him like a transformation scene, away almost to the stormy wall of Wales. It was as if he were riding further and further westward, following towards the sunset the road of the fallen kings; where a low red light glows forever upon things forgotten amid the last ruins of the Round Table. And yet I am not sure of such a view of history; it seems to me that with us also things change and even change places; and the war does not always go one way. When I used to go out as a boy into the green twilight, having written nonsense all night (fortunately unpublished), and drink coffee at a stall in the street, brooding upon all these things, it seemed then as if the tide were running high enough in the one direction; but I have since had a notion that high tides can turn. The enormous buildings, seen in outline like uncouth drawings, seem to stand up more insecurely against an altered sky; with some change in it too subtle yet to be called the twilight. I discovered, at least, that even in all that labyrinth of the new London by night there is an unvisited hour of almost utter stillness, before the creaking carts begin to come in from the market-gardens, to remind us that there is still somewhere a countryside. And in that stillness I have sometimes fancied I heard, tiny and infinitely far away, something like a faint voice hallooing and the sound of horse hoofs that return.

G K Chesterton

Autobiography

In *Autobiography* Chesterton describes his happy childhood, the intellectual 'doubts and morbidities' of his youth and his search for a true vocation.

He includes many anecdotes about his literary friends, Henry James, George Bernard Shaw and H G Wells.

But it is his quest for religious conviction and his conversion to Catholicism that is central to his story which he tells with great modesty, gentleness and intelligence.

Chaucer

Chesterton expounds the 'genius of Geoffrey Chaucer' in this literary biography that explores both the writer and his time. He claims that Chaucer and his Age were 'more sane, more normal and more cheerful than writers that came after him' and the characters he portrayed have an immediate contemporary relevance.

Beautifully and sensitively written, this biography about the 'Father of English Poetry' will inform and inspire.

G K CHESTERTON

CRITICISMS AND APPRECIATIONS OF THE WORKS OF CHARLES DICKENS

Written with intelligence and authority, these twenty-three essays provide an insight into the works of the literary genius of Charles Dickens.

Chesterton greatly admired Dickens as a social prophet and defender of the common man. Here, he focuses both on the style and the ideology of Dickens and provides the critical insight into his work with his characteristic perceptive generosity. Chesterton is still regarded by many as one of the most accomplished and perceptive critics of Dickens.

As much about Chesterton's strongly held beliefs as about Dickens, this volume is sure to inform and give pleasure to advocates of both writers.

GEORGE BERNARD SHAW

The book traces in some detail Shaw's work as a critic (puritanical opposition to Shakespeare) and as a dramatist.

Chesterton was ideally placed to write this critical biography of the literary works and political views of George Bernard Shaw. He was a personal friend and yet an ardent opponent of Shaw's progressive socialism. The lightness of tone and the humour of his other works are equally present in his examination of Shaw. The book presents a perceptive and far from dated critique of Shaw's philosophy and politics and, through them, the emerging progressive orthodoxy of the 20th century.

The book represents an excellent introduction to Shaw's work and the spirit of the age in which it was created.

Printed in Great Britain
by Amazon

49564018R00057